Mountain Majesty
A History of CODEP Haiti Volume 1

Doug & Bibb —

Such a joy to meet you
and want to thank you
for your interest in and
support for CODEP.

Grace & Peace
John Winings

Mountain Majesty

The History of CODEP Haiti
Where Sustainable Agricultural
Development Works

Volume I

John V. Winings

Dudley Court Press
Sonoita AZ

Published in the United States of America by:

Dudley Court Press
PO Box 102
Sonoita, AZ 85637 USA

www.DudleyCourtPress.com

Paperback ISBN: 9781940013213
Kindle ISBN: 9781940013220
Epub ISBN: 9781940013237
Hardcover ISBN: 9781940013244

LCCN: 2016930151

Publisher's Cataloging-in-Publication Data

Names: Winings, John V., author.
Title: Mountain majesty : the history of CODEP Haiti where sustainable agricultural development
          works / John V. Winings.
Description: Sonoita, AZ : Dudley Court Press, [2016] | Includes bibliographical references
          and index.
Identifiers: ISBN: 978-1-940013-21-3 (paperback) | 978-1-940013-24-4 (hardcover) |
          978-1-940012-22-0 (Kindle) | 978-1-940013-23-7 (epub)
Subjects: LCSH: CODEP Haiti--History. | Sustainable agriculture--Haiti. | Reforestation--Haiti. | Soil
          conservation--Haiti. | Agricultural development projects--Haiti. | Rural development projects
          --Haiti. | Economic development projects--Haiti. | Nonprofit organizations-- Haiti--History. |
          Church charities--Haiti--History. | Missions--Haiti--History.
Classification: LCC: S477.H2 W56 2016 | DDC: 630.68/07294--dc23

Photo on page 45 courtesy of Diana Bedoya

All other photos courtesy of Deborah Winings

Connect with John Winings at *www.JohnWinings.com*

This book is dedicated to Debbie and Emma,
whose understanding and help throughout
its writing and editing cannot be stated
emphatically enough.

Contents

Foreword

I first met John Winings in 2011 when he came to visit me at Duke University, where I then codirected the Haiti Laboratory at the Franklin Humanities Center. Along with my colleague Deborah Jenson, I launched this laboratory in 2010, just months after the earthquake that had devastated the country, and our goal was to connect humanistic research on the history and culture of Haiti with the work being done in law, health, and the environment in the country. From our first meeting, I was struck by Winings' remarkable knowledge and commitment in confronting one of the fundamental challenges facing Haiti today: that of deforestation, and its impact on the environment and therefore on the lives and livelihoods of rural Haitians.

My conversations with John encouraged me to organize a series of workshops around the topic of the environment in Haiti, in which we brought together Haitian and U.S. scholars with practitioners. The work of CODEP became a centerpiece of these discussions, as we learned about how the project had evolved over the decades through constant interaction with and response to the social and cultural context they encountered. What struck me and other participants in these workshops about the work of CODEP was the extent to which it had become intertwined with the practices and aspirations of the rural communities of which it is a part.

There are thousands of NGOs working in Haiti today. And yet it is surprisingly difficult to get a holistic sense of what they do and how well their projects work. This is a serious problem, for it is difficult to evaluate and analyze the ultimate impact of such organizations without such empirical knowledge. In this book, Winings offers us a very valuable account of the work of CODEP. As a historian of Haiti, I particularly appreciate the fact that this account provides us a longer-term perspective on how the organization evolved, on the dialogues and contingencies that shaped its work, and on the way practice coalesced through negotiation and trial and error.

The critical insight that has driven CODEP's work is that any contribution to the environmental and agricultural situation in Haiti needs to be conceived of at the level of a watershed. This holistic approach, in which forests are understood not just as part of a broader ecosystem but also as a foundation for a set of social and economic practices and networks, is vital. And it is something that other organizations, in Haiti and beyond, could learn from.

CODEP's story, as told here, is a vital reminder of the power and necessity of listening and observing, of the rich foundations Haitian society itself offers up for the cultivation of alternative futures, and of the centrality and beauty of our remarkable—though so often mistreated—companions: trees and forests.

Laurent Dubois, PhD
Duke University

Preface

This book records the history of the Comprehensive Development Project (CODEP) in the mountains south of Léogâne, Haiti. Over the past twenty-five years, CODEP has become one of the more successful agriculture development projects in Haiti, and perhaps in the world.

There are two distinct periods in the life of CODEP. During the first, Jack Hanna was the visionary and Rodney Babe the project designer and implementer. Both were essential in making CODEP what it is today. Their story of how the project came to be is a fascinating one and fills this book. The second volume tells how CODEP fared after both of them left.

After working in Haiti Fund for ten years and having my life significantly altered by the experience, I have tried to capture in this book what makes this sustainable agricultural development project so special. I've tried to reflect the facts accurately, even when stories are in conflict with each other because different people tell them with different reflections and different interpretations. Such is the nature of humans. I've attempted here to view the material broadly, and not reflect only one perspective. Add to this the nuances of the culture of Haiti and a different language, and the story becomes fascinating; I hope you find it so also.

The story of CODEP is also a composite of many moving stories of individual lives. I have included three of them as a way to weave the tapestry that makes this project so very human. You have here the stories of Jean Clement Tercelin, Joseph Edvy Durandice, and Larose Marie Carmella, whom everyone calls Nwèl.

Rather than create a day-by-day chronology, I felt it more helpful to look at broad trends, significant mistakes, and important learnings that helped make CODEP a success. Sustainable agricultural development works this way—hit or miss, retrench and learn, move forward, find success—even in small doses. You will find this bumpy road here. I've included appendices with a chronological timeline, and one that includes a glossary of terms. You thus can keep track of the dates, acronyms, and names.

Because Haitian Creole is of French derivation and is a newly written language, there are many choices when spelling different words. This can be frustrating for outsiders. I will dip you into this pool of uncertainty: throughout the book, you will be exposed to French, Kreyòl, and English spellings of words. It is like this when you live in Haiti day to day. I hope this gives you a sense of the richness of Haitian culture, language, and history.

Notes are one of my favorite ways to explain nuances in a narrative, to promote understanding and to provide background. Accordingly, throughout the book you will find many comments, sources, and references. If you choose not to read them, fine, but know the story continues before and after.

Finally, this book describes what makes CODEP unique and special in the midst of roughly ten thousand other NGOs (nongovernmental organizations) operating in Haiti, both rural and urban. I have not tried to paint a picture of Haiti and other NGOs outside of my particular experiences in and near Léogâne. I have witnessed lives being changed every day in that incredible sustainable agricultural development project called CODEP.

Acknowledgments

This book could not have been written without the support and encouragement of many people. Becky Christian, a clear thinker and editor, had many helpful comments. Also, Jim Sylivant, an engineer, went through everything at least once, finding typos and asking key questions of understanding. My wife Debbie, with lots of things on her plate, was steadfast and supportive, reading several versions of chapters, rewrites, and extraneous material that didn't make the book. Without their constant encouragement, good humor, and support, this book would never have made it to print.

John Thienpont, Martha Johnson, Bill Hathaway, Laurent Dubois, Winston Dixon, Bob Herrick, and others helped in ways too numerous to iterate here. I am especially indebted to the board of directors of Haiti Fund, Inc., who gave me open access to all their archives, records, and photos of the early project. Publisher Gail Woodard, copy editor Pam Nordberg, and the Dudley Court Press taught me the ways of modern publishing and without whom, who knows what would have been the outcome.

But, the real thanks goes to those Haitians who have made CODEP what it is today. Through leadership, courage, understanding, patience, and hard work they have helped bring the story of their sustainable development project to these pages. Among those involved were the CODEP animators and chèf ekips, folks at APKF, and others. Special thanks go to Edvy Durandice, Clement Tercelin, and Nwèl, whose real name is Larose Marie Carmella, for allowing me to put their stories in these pages to bring the human side to this book.

Finally, I owe Jack Hanna a large debt of gratitude for encouraging me to write this history. He died before one final interview we had scheduled. But the story doesn't change. CODEP people wrote this moving tribute to his vision and leadership, which was lovingly read at his memorial service:

7 February 2014

For the family of Jack Hanna

From the Committee of the Director of CODEP, and all the animators, and the entire 1404 members who work in CODEP:

We all together were really sorry when we heard the bad news about Jack's death. Because Jack, in 1989, planted a spiritual tree called CODEP in the Cormier (core me yea) valley, that tree which grew to four other sections of the county of Léogâne where now, in the year 2014, there are thousands of people who benefit indirectly. We are reaping these fruits from the spiritual tree that is CODEP, which Jack planted in the Cormier valley.

It is for this reason that we ask God to make a place for Jack in paradise, and to permit Jesus Christ to find a place for Jack in Heaven. And we pray for the family and for God to give them strength during this untimely death.

And (we ask) that God to care for him, because we must always bless his name.

On behalf of the committee of the Director of CODEP

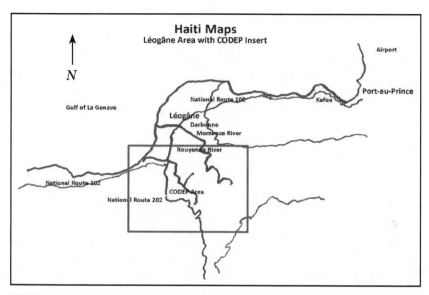

Haiti Maps
Léogâne Area with CODEP Insert

Airport

Port-au-Prince

National Route 102

Gulf of La Gonave

Léogâne

Darbonne

Momence River

Kafou

Rouyonne River

National Route 102

National Route 202

CODEP Area

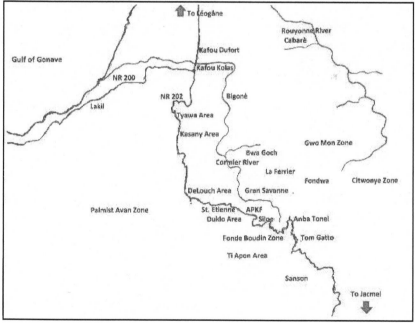

To Léogâne

Rouyonne River

Cabarè

Kafou Dufort

Kafou Kolas

Gulf of Gonave

NR 200

NR 202

Bigonè

Lakil

Tyawa Area

Kasany Area

Gwo Mon Zone

Bwa Goch

Cormier River

La Fervier

Fondwa

Citwonye Zone

DeLouch Area

Gran Savanne

Palmist Avan Zone

St. Etienne   APKf

Dukdo Area   Silos   Anba Tonel

Fonde Boudin Zone   Tom Gatto

Ti Apon Area

Sanson

To Jacmel

The Footpath . . .

Maybe it was just seeing the friendly new home painted green and yellow, with small but inviting bunks. Or maybe it was the exhaustion from trekking up and down the hills of Haiti to get here. But, more likely, it was the combination of heat, humidity, sweat, and aching muscles that made us sleep for twelve hours.

It was March 2006. Jamie Rhoads, a CODEP intern whom we had known ten years earlier when we advised the Presbytery Youth Council, was showing us the mission project called CODEP (Comprehensive Development Project). This was my second trip to Haiti, and my wife Debbie's first. We had flown from Raleigh-Durham airport that morning, connecting in Miami with the short hour-and-twenty-minute flight to Port-au-Prince. That's when the cultural shocks began.

In those days there were no jet ramps; you descended to the tarmac on stairways perched on a pickup truck. The first sensation was the overwhelming heat, wind, and dust. The second was the brightness of the day, the sun hot on your head and face as you looked out at the tarmac.

It was a time of political upheaval in Haiti. In February two years earlier, President Jean-Bertrand Aristide had been evacuated—resigned for his own safety or pushed out by his enemies, including the US government, depending on who is telling the story. After Aristide flew out of Haiti on US government aircraft, a UN task force called MINUSTAH sent between five- and eight-thousand troops from Korea, Brazil, Sri Lanka, and other countries.

The UN asked the chief justice of the Haitian Supreme Court to take the presidency on an interim basis until free and fair elections could elect a new president. Those elections didn't occur until May 2006, so the election season was in full stride when we were there.*

A lot of literature exists on this period in Haiti's history. Aristide was first elected president of Haiti in 1990, installed with great hoopla in February 1991, but was deposed in a coup d'état seven months later. After two years, he was reinstated and finished his five-year term after returning from exile. Reelected again in 2000 under a cloud of election fraud accusations, his second term had many of the same problems. (For more on this topic, you can find a thorough discussion of those times in Haiti in a book by Peter Hallward, 2007, Damming the Flood: Haiti, Aristide, and the Politics of Containment. *London: Verso Books. p. 210. ISBN 1-84467-106-2.)*

The Presbyterian Church (PCUSA) had pulled all missionaries out of Haiti the prior June, including the directors of CODEP, Rodney and Sharyn Babe, whom Jamie had worked with for two years. By now the political situation had relaxed to the point where, with care, it was reasonably safe for us to travel to Haiti.

Jamie had arranged for all three of us to take an MAF flight from the Port-au-Prince domestic air terminal to Jacmel on the south coast of Haiti. (MAF is Mission Aviation Fellowship—a Florida organization that uses small planes to fly missionaries into remote areas.) Jamie's plane was late arriving from New York. So when Debbie and I got to Port-au-Prince, we were met by Limose Murat, an English-speaking Haitian man who was the head transportation guy for the Episcopal Bishop of Haiti.

Although the domestic terminal was close by on the airport grounds, it was necessary to exit the airport and take a taxi the half-mile distance between them. But because security was important, Mr. Murat arranged for us to take a taxi with a known and trusted driver. He also told us how much the fare should be so we wouldn't have an argument when we arrived.

We piled into a beat-up old vehicle with our bags and backpacks and drove out of the airport. The city was quite a shock to both of us. Traffic was loud, dusty, congested, and interspersed with street vendors, in the middle of the street as well as on the sides—destitute, starving little ruffian boys who were begging for money, pecking on the window, rubbing their stomachs, and looking pleadingly into our eyes. Others were selling everything imaginable from rolled-up artwork on canvases without frames to chunks of food of unknown origin or safety.

Occasional fetid pools of "water" lined the road, along with plastic bottles, Styrofoam remnants of food trays, shipping foam and peanuts, plus shoes and rags—all in the soup. Torn black polyethylene bags skipped along in the wind, often dragged down into the glop. An acrid stench of exhaust smoke, foul-smelling decay, and human waste carried along by the hot, dry wind seemed to permeate everything.

Poverty was everywhere. People without limbs or with severe disabilities were limping along or sitting right on the ground. Many of them hawked everything from watches to phone-charging cigarette-lighter plug-ins, plus large cardboard cones with unknown, unlabeled pills taped to the outside for anyone who wanted to buy something for a perceived or real malady of one sort or another.

Others were selling drinks of questionable palatability, but most were shouting, "*Dlo, dlo, dlo,*" which we learned is the word for water. In French, water is *eau* often preceded by *le, la,* or *de.* In Haiti, it is all run together as *dlo.* The short distance on the road between the two entrances to the airport took about fifteen minutes to drive because of the severe congestion. An overwhelming fifteen minutes in a cacophony of horns, shouts, blaring radios, and vendor hawkers—which we now know is the crushing and closely packed hordes that are urban Haiti.

At the domestic terminal, we were introduced to the American pilot, who spent about half his time in Haiti flying various people around the country. Ours was a short flight, and inexpensive, but the pilot was a bit nervous. Jamie was running late, and the plane had to go to Jacmel, deliver us, and return before dark to Port-au-Prince, as the airport does not have landing lights!

Finally, Jamie arrived. We loaded our bags and taxied out to the runway. The Port-au-Prince airport has one runway. Period. No taxiways. All planes enter the gate area from a single taxi ramp going to each of the two terminals. To take off, a plane goes out to the runway, taxis to the end, turns around on a specially made turning "circle," guns the engines, and takes off. Same with MAF, but with a small plane and the wind from the west he just turned, we roared down the runway, and off we went.

We flew for about twenty minutes to Jacmel on the south coast. Jamie pointed to sections of CODEP that we could see. The differences were stark—areas of dark green dense forest, and lighter green patches with new trees. Around these CODEP areas were huge patches of completely barren land—no trees, huge gullies, no soil—obviously incapable of sustaining life, plant or animal. This was our first birds-eye view of the contrast between how things were before CODEP and what they had become with CODEP's involvement.

As we approached the airstrip, we could see the barrenness of the land around Jacmel—treeless mounds of stark, light-brown and gray humps of land, with huge washouts in the dry riverbed. The river flowing into the Jacmel Harbor is deeply gouged out and quite wide, as much as five hundred meters in some places. We could see the nearly dry river snaking off to the right toward the harbor as we made a direct downhill approach to the runway.

We felt an abrupt jolt as the plane landed. Jacmel is one of about fifteen Haitian airports that has "paved" runways. Paved is a loose definition here, as most are not much more than thin tarmac, a couple of inches of asphalt over a flat dirt strip. The runway is about three thousand feet long. I understand it is one of the better runways; Jacmel is an artists' community, a beach city. Many wealthy Haitians from Port-au-Prince and New York maintain homes here. Apparently they have some influence on the quality of the airport runway.

Clement, Mimi, and Edvy were waiting for us after having traveled over the mountain in the CODEP pickup. These men's names were among the many we would learn in CODEP, as others had done over the years. They were happy to see us, and upon Jamie's advice, we stopped for a late lunch at a local restaurant. (It was about four o'clock, and Jamie knew none of them had eaten anything all day—though they would not have mentioned it.)

We climbed into the back of the pickup to ride, standing. On the ride up we could more easily see the mountain ridge to the other coast of the southern "thumb" of Haiti, some sixty-five kilometers away. The wind rushed against our faces and sunglasses, hats tied down or worn backward.

We saw what seemed like rubble everywhere: piles of limestone at various points along the road, as well as concrete block houses and storefronts with reinforcing bar sticking out the top of nearly all of them.*

The limestone piles are sand used in making concrete blocks (one at a time in a two-piece mold) for sale or construction. Because the currency is unstable, people convert discretionary cash into an asset; a pile of sand has a stable value. The reason for the protruding rebar is that once a house is finished, you have to pay government taxes, so very few houses are ever "finished."

There were street vendors everywhere, even out and away from Jacmel. Every mile or so were a cluster of houses and stores close to the road with signs for the lottery. Everywhere the lottery takes money from those who can least afford it, who are betting on long odds, hoping to hit it big and make their lives easier.

At various places, you can see far into the hills. On the uphill trek from Jacmel, the land is dry and parched. Limestone subsoil protrudes everywhere and there are a few hardy bushes or trees, but mostly it looks like a barren, hilly desert without the plants you see in the American southwest. Occasionally you can see the river with huge piles of washed-down rock debris from floods.

When we reached the top of the hill, it had begun to grow dark. The dusk is very short in the tropics. Soon there were small fires dotting the road on both sides with people sitting close behind them—another new experience, as our concern was for their safety from traffic—but they (and the passing vehicles) hardly seemed to notice.

We learned later that the topography begins to change at the top of the hill. Although there are barren patches in the distance, the roadsides are mostly covered with trees. You don't see nearly the same amounts of erosion. CODEP's reforestation has had a profound impact on the ecology of the region. It is barren from Jacmel to the top because CODEP hasn't yet begun working in that area.

We arrived "home" an hour later and ate a fabulous meal of colored rice (called *diri kolè*), Congo beans (or pigeon peas), fried plantain patties, and *pikliz*. A kind of coleslaw, pikliz is made with finely sliced cabbage, carrots, and vile-hot peppers that are exactly the same color as the carrots. Cook Madame* Gabriel cooked this over a propane stove. The secret is to use lots of garlic and *maggi* cubes, bouillon-sized cubes that are nearly 100% monosodium glutamate. Not good for the heart or keeping blood pressure low, but fabulous after a long, famished day of an assault on your senses.

Women in Haiti are known by their husband's name, a cultural nuance that speaks of the patriarchal society. I have since found it is more of a convention than a real cultural more, as rural women have considerable power and responsibility.

Then we went to bed, exhausted and overwhelmed by the sensory overload of all we had seen since we arrived in Port-au-Prince. We slept well, ceiling fans blowing hard to keep off the mosquitoes and sweat. We fell asleep listening to the traffic, with horns blaring on the road on one side of the guesthouse, and the soft lapping of the waves outside on the other.

Up early the next morning, we made some stops on the way up the hill to see the project. The first stop was at APKF, a farmers' co-op that does microlending and provides a farm store, to see Edvy again and thank him for coming to meet us in Jacmel.

We also visited with Pastor Dures, the headmaster of the Siloe School, an institution supported by CODEP. Dures is a leader in the project and also the school's headmaster, teaching CODEP agricultural techniques to the kids. Each year they germinate seeds in plastic bags and water them every day for six months. Grown into seedlings, they are replanted on May 1, National Agriculture Day in Haiti.

Teachers teach classes at the school mostly by rote. Students have uniforms unique to that school, and they are shiny-faced and bright-eyed, always happy to see new *blans* (whites or foreigners). We realized later their joy was over the chance to see Jamie, who had lived there for two years.

The school had nine classes, each about fifteen to twenty kids and each with a "professor" usually wearing dress pants and a tie. Pastè Dures was there to greet us. Pastè is often the name for leaders, whether they are real pastors or not; in Dures's case, he had a church right at the school. Teachers teach classes in Kreyòl and sometimes French, and students studied math, reading, history, civics, and agriculture.

In Haiti, almost all of the schools are private. Only a few government-owned schools exist, and by American standards, they are hardly adequate. Schools have no textbooks and few blackboards or chalk, so rote learning is a necessity, regardless of how slow and tedious it is.

After having coffee and bread—a tradition in Haiti for guests—we went back up to the top of the hill and were dropped off at Anba Tonel. In this small community the main footpath leads down to Bwa Goch, where Jamie had lived and where we would spend the night.

As is often the case with Americans, we didn't start our trek till nearly one thirty p.m. The Haitian workday starts early, continues mostly without breaks, but ends before the real heat of the day becomes oppressive. Our late departure time meant we would do our hike with the Haitian heat bearing down on us. But we had plenty of drinking water and snacks to give us energy.

We learned some things on the way: It is harder going downhill than uphill. During the dry season, tiny bits of dirt accumulate on the pathways and become very slick (*glisè* in Kreyòl). So you have to watch very carefully that you don't slide and fall, or worse, pitch forward and fall. Going uphill is hard on your heart but there is a shorter distance to fall, and shortness of breath keeps you at a reasonable pace. The trick when ascending is to have the lead (faster) people wait till you catch up and then wait some more. That way the slowest ones have completely caught their breath. Start sooner and the slower ones never catch their breath and lose stamina.

As a consequence of having two older, out-of-shape blans along, it took us till about five p.m. to reach Bwa Goch that day. Madame Philip and Philip were excited to have us and to see Jamie again after almost a year. Jamie also could see "Ti Jamie" (little Jamie), Philip and his wife's son who was born before Jamie was living there but who had acquired the nickname when Jamie arrived. Jamie had lived in the yellow and green pastel *gwo kay* (large house) that Madame Philip had earned from working in CODEP.

These houses are built from treated wood shipped in from the USA. Treating makes the wood resistant to insects, especially termites, so they are quite useful for housing. Concrete block houses are preferred but are not possible at such a distance from the road, so the wood gwo kays are appreciated. The house was twelve feet by twenty feet of living space with two rooms, a large door at both ends, and windows placed on the long sides, plus a four-foot overhang on one end for a porch. Jamie told us we would sleep in the room with the two wood-frame beds, while he would use the floor of the "living" room.

Madame Philip had prepared us black beans and rice, and we went to her house with walls constructed of wooden poles and slabs that were heavy and nailed into place. Her roof also was made of metal, perhaps at one time galvanized, but now rusty, thin, and held in place with large rocks on top. She had a small table, and everyone crowded around to eat, talk, and laugh—even shy Ti Jamie.

On the way into Bwa Goch earlier, we had met a Haitian man dressed in a brown suit and tie, on his way to preach a funeral for someone in the Bwa Goch community. We marveled at how, in a suit and tie, he barely broke a sweat in the heat and afternoon sun. The wake was that evening, with the funeral the next day. Jamie told us he felt obligated to go to the wake, as we would leave long before the funeral the next morning.

After dinner, he gave us a flashlight and headed to the wake, telling us we could find our way back to his house by following the footpath. We understood the reason for the flashlight when we stepped outside into total, complete darkness. Trees covered the entire area over the path; it was a moonless night. We took turns with the flashlight, I in the lead, going three or four steps, then turning the flashlight behind me to light the path so Debbie could catch up. Then I'd go a few more steps, all of this on a narrow path carved along a steep hillside.

After about four turns of our flashlight protocol, we heard a soft voice say, "*Excizim*," the Kreyòl word for "excuse me." Here was a young girl not more than fourteen or fifteen walking toward us on the path, whom we obviously hadn't seen and would have crashed right into. It wouldn't have been a problem for her, but she was walking along in the pitch dark carrying a five-gallon bucket of water on her head!

With no flashlight and no light of any kind, her eyes were obviously accustomed to the dark. Of course, our flashlight had nearly caused her to lose her night vision, but she was close enough to home to be OK. We laughed embarrassedly as we sidled past each other, the bucket of water never flinching nor a drop of water jostling out. Amazing.

We got to the cabin, pulled back the thin sheets on the hard bed, and prepared to go to sleep. It was about six thirty p.m. We were totally

The Footpath . . .

exhausted but filled with joy and appreciation for the new experiences in a part of God's world unknown to us before.

Debbie shined the light around the room, noticing a large burlap bag filled with peanuts drying for the market. On top was a huge spider, maybe four inches across. It slowly moved away from the bed, exiting over the side of the bag and down toward the floor. We were so tired that we decided everyone needed to sleep, spider included. We each took a bed, laid down, pulled up the covers, and promptly fell into a deep, exhausted sleep.

The next morning it got light about six a.m., so we soon were up to see what the new day would bring. Madame Philip had earned a cistern from CODEP that roof rainwater drained into. There was still enough water in it at the end of the dry season so that we could splash a bit of water on our faces to greet the day. It is amazing how refreshing cold water on a cool, humid morning feels.

Debbie told me that she had been up in the night. She had needed to urinate, so she took the flashlight and went outside to find a spot. Just as she started, she heard a deep sigh and realized that there was an animal or a person close by. She had two choices: turn the flashlight on and bring attention to herself, or leave it off and take her chances. She left it off and toughed it out, slipping back inside as another sigh came. Looking out the next morning, she realized it was a tethered cow, who had been either grazing or sleeping and had awakened when Debbie invaded her territory!

That morning we headed off to meet and stay with Madame Jacques. When we were ready to leave, Debbie was surprised and thrilled to see Madame Inez, one of the CODEP leaders. She had hiked three miles from the main road and arrived well before eight o'clock. During the day, she insisted on carrying Debbie's backpack, which was a much-needed respite for Debbie.

We headed for the home of Madame Jacques, also a CODEP worker. Her house was on the crest of a ridge and looked out toward Léogâne, with a most spectacular view of the city, the ocean beyond, and the island of La Gonave in the distance.

We had a bit of an easier trek the second day, as we started early. *Gwo Mon* (large mountain) is a large mountain, as the name implies, so we were pretty tired when we arrived. We still were able to appreciate the view, but we again would sleep well. They insisted we take the room with the bed and they would sleep on the floor. Jamie told us we should accept the offer; not to do so might offend.

Soon after we arrived, Jamie had fallen into deep conversation with Madame Jacques. I knew it needn't concern us because I could read the body language of both of them. Madame Jacques was sad because her son had been killed just two days earlier in Port-au-Prince. A huge issue in Haiti is convincing young people that it is better for them to stay in the rural areas than to go to Port-au-Prince where life is much more on the edge. They want to find a job with good pay and thereby gain access to all the music, shopping, and lifestyle that a big city has to offer.

Madame Jacques's home, traditional with rustic, uneven wood sideboards and homemade chairs in the gallerie, or porch, for taking in the superb view from the mountain and socializing in the evenings, a cultural norm lost to most Americans today.

Unfortunately, innocent rural kids become targets for the criminal element. Madame Jacques's son had convinced a taxi owner to let him take the night shift. He apparently drove into a vile area and was shot as he drove, looking for an address. Madame Jacques did not know more of the specifics, but her sadness showed in her every move.

But we saw in her a certain stoicism that we would soon learn is characteristic of the Haitians. They know how to grieve, accept what life deals them with strong faith, understand the new realities, and get on with life. Americans should have a chance to see these human feelings displayed firsthand.

After dinner, we looked at several political posters tacked up along a series of tree trunks lining the footpath in front of Madame Jacques's home. The election cycle was in full swing, and the polls would eventually elect René Preval on May 14th, 2006, who had once before followed Aristide (in 1996) to a second term.

Madame Jacques had a small generator and a radio, which was broadcasting a long series of discussions about the political candidates. The election season has not only open and frank conversation among the candidates, but also political riots and violent demonstrations. A system like this would not appeal to either Americans or Canadians, I suspect, but is one that seems to work for Haiti.

The next morning we walked all the way down through Gwo Mon to the Rouyonne River, where our driver Mimi met us. You might wonder how/why Mimi met us in a river? When we were there, at the end of the dry season, the Rouyonne, which runs down the mountain gullies to and through Leyogàn, is an almost completely dry, wide riverbed.

However, during the rainy season, it becomes a fierce river, with floods easily overflowing the banks and inundating all the surrounding area. The losses include sugar cane fields, gardens, houses, animals, and sometimes people from the onrushing water, which can rise and flood with only a few minutes warning.

As we completed this trek, Debbie's first trip became one for her record book and journal. There was only one problem. When it came time to go home, she wanted to stay. Captivated by the people, their incredible spirit and élan, she felt this was a wonderful refuge from the hurried pace and consumer-driven mentality in the USA.

Too often, even in our churches, there seems to be little appreciation for the amount of suffering and poverty existing so close to our borders. In Haiti, the people in the mountains south of Léogâne had ground out their livelihoods from nothing at all. I soon learned much of this was a result of the organization called Haiti Fund/CODEP.

Debbie is fond of saying, "A visit to Haiti leaves you changed for the rest of your life." What wonder is this country of Haiti with its amazing contrasts and starkness! Indescribable poverty, but joyful hope and strong spiritual beliefs.

So, in those few days of March 2006, we found that the work of CODEP continued in spite of Rodney and Sharyn's removal by the church for security reasons eight months earlier. They didn't know when they would be allowed to come back, and they stayed in close touch with the project through telephone calls and an occasional email from friends.

This first chapter describes for you a midpoint in the CODEP project, a point where we can look back on the rationale, history, and incredible story that lies behind the Comprehensive Development Project in all its many aspects.

How this all became possible must begin with the inception of the project in the mind of its founder some twenty years earlier.

Chapter 2

Jack Hanna, the Visionary

The Comprehensive Development Project (CODEP) exists today because of the vision and resourcefulness of a man named Jack Hanna. John P. Hanna retired from General Electric in Connecticut as a research executive. He jumped at the opportunity to retire early in 1982 at age fifty-eight. He and his wife, Evelyn, decided to flee Connecticut and its cold winters. They planned to summer at their place in New Hampshire and winter in the South.

They had a hard time finding the right wintering spot. Florida beckoned, particularly northeast Florida, near Jacksonville. Research showed there had been few hurricanes in the previous fifty years, and lots of lovely golf courses abounded. Best of all, excellent medical facilities were on the horizon, as a new Mayo Clinic was set to open in 1986. They ruled out other sites as too humid or too hot. Eventually, Jack and Evelyn decided to keep all the choices open and buy a boat.

They studied up, bought an elegant Taiwan-built oceangoing trawler, and spent a year fitting it up to their liking. When it was ready, they cruised down the Intracoastal Waterway, stopping in New Bern, North Carolina, to winter. They began to plan how to both enjoy the fun of retirement and also to do volunteer work.

The Hannas joined the First Presbyterian Church of New Bern. Jack inquired about volunteer work in the Caribbean, calling David Young, who was the head of development mission for the Presbyterian Church in the US (PCUS), headquartered in Atlanta. Hanna's summer church in New Hampshire was a Methodist Church, so they inquired at its national headquarters also. This was a dead end—Jack didn't have the required master's of divinity degree. In the meantime, they worked on the boat.

Preparing a boat to cruise ocean waters is no simple task. Redundant systems, offshore equipment, safety gear, and provisions are the broad categories, with innumerable details in each. Each must be itemized, purchased, checked, and rechecked. It took another year to be ready, but they finally began to fulfill their dreams. A couple of years cruising the islands would be fun and still leave time to volunteer. Life was comfortable and not very hard. They were building lots of memories and stories to tell their grandchildren. This was the prize of Jack's years of hard work at GE.

One day they were in Barbados, the easternmost of the Caribbean islands. They moored the boat at a luxury marina—planning to stay for several weeks. They could cruise nearby and enjoy the warmth of the winter sun. A long walk on the sandy beach would be a great way to start the current odyssey.

They started off at a brisk pace one crystal morning. They walked about a mile down the beach, well past the security gate that kept the riffraff away from the marina. A native woman with several small children and a tiny infant came out of the dense forest and walked right up to Evelyn.

Somewhat taken aback, she said, "May I help you?"

The woman, in a torrent of hard-to-understand English, said, "You are rich Americans. You have plenty of food. You live a good life. Please take my child. He will starve if you don't take him. I can't begin to feed my family, and he is such a lovely child. Won't you please take him and give him a better life?"

Of course, Jack and Evelyn were not able to take the child. Even if they had decided to do so, the regulations on adoption within the legal system of Barbados would have been nearly impossible. Plus, now in their sixties, how could they possibly be good parents to a still-nursing infant?

But this incident profoundly changed both their lives. They had long, agonizing discussions questioning what the purpose of life was. So Jack and Evelyn changed their plans radically. Jack put it this way to me years later:* "What were we doing cruising around the Caribbean when there was such poverty and so many people who were malnourished and unhealthy? Why should we be so special?

Much of the information contained in this and other chapters was developed in a series of conversations with Jack over a three-year period late in his life at a Presbyterian assisted-living facility in Laurinburg, NC.

"What had God done to us? And why did we happen to be the couple that woman approached? What were we supposed to do, anyway? This incident threw much cold water on our plans for leisurely growing old together. We had to do something. The task seemed insurmountable. How could we even understand the conditions around the problem? If this was the situation in Barbados, which is fairly affluent comparatively, what must other islands in the Caribbean be like? All these questions haunted us for weeks."

Jack wanted to get back to the US and research the problem. What kinds of organizations already were in place to help? What role might Evelyn and he play? They took the boat back north, again to New Bern. They would live on the boat until they decided how best to proceed.

Jack talked to David Young in Atlanta a second time. The Presbyterians didn't do mission work directly in the Caribbean. In Jamaica, a Swiss organization called the Institute for Cultural Affairs (ICA) had already contacted the PCUS. As a result, David Young had an interest in doing a project there.

The ICA approach was to work with poor communities who had land but didn't have the skills, organization, or money to accomplish economic development. Trained leaders were needed so they could manage the project in a year or two.

Since Jack hadn't yet settled on a permanent residence, they could go to Kingston, live on the boat, and help get things started in Jamaica. Jamaica was a nice country, the residents spoke English, and the Jamaican government wanted to work with ICA to develop several communities. Jack and Evelyn were convinced.

David Young was supportive of their efforts. He put them in contact with people in the Caribbean—a doctor who ran a hospital in Haiti and an ICA office in Jamaica. Some young Jamaicans were working with sixteen villages in the Blue Mountains in Eastern Jamaica that had common interests, attitudes, procedures, and continuity. The president of ICA Jamaica was interested in having the outside help.

Many administrative procedures had yet to be worked out with the government. ICA in the states had not worked with bureaucratic governments. Jack, therefore, spent part of every week going from department to department in Kingston to complete all the permits. In the mountains, he and Evelyn assessed each organization. They also wanted a sense of each village's hopes and desires. The project must fit the culture or it is not likely to work; the economic plans and ideas need to match what the communities want to do.

The largest and most key village was Woburn Lawn. Jack and Evelyn stayed there when they went up to the Blue Mountains. ICA had already set up offices in Woburn Lawn. Jack and Evelyn had vehicles, a driver, and soon they found a small cottage in the mountains and moored the boat at the Royal Jamaican Yacht Club. With these arrangements made, Jack was happy.

The Jamaican government, though bureaucratic, had good records. Therefore, the villages could gain clear title to land. Getting the administrative paperwork done was a tedious task, but once complete, each village had long-term land rights conveyed. Large coffee plantations operated all around them, so it was natural for the communities to cooperate and grow coffee for sale.

Many community residents worked on the coffee plantations already but had no ownership or participation in the profits. However, Jack encouraged them to continue working on the plantations while they began growing coffee on land they owned. Taking the brand name Blue Mountain Coffee (BMC) and getting enthusiastic support from the communities made it clear that this was the opportunity ICA had been seeking.*

---

*Should you want more reading about ICA and its community development work, see METHODS FOR COMMUNITY DEVELOPMENT: THE WORK OF THE INSTITUTE OF CULTURAL AFFAIRS by Stuart A. Umpleby, Department of Management Science, The George Washington University, Washington, DC 20052, umpleby@gwu.edu.

Jack helped residents form an economic development corporation (EDC) licensed by the government. The local members of the EDC began to plant coffee on family-owned land. A joint coffee-planting effort interested many peasants. But the total area the peasants owned was far too small to provide sufficient quantities of coffee to support all the communities.

The residents had no capital, so Jack helped them organize the Blue Mountain Development Corporation as a stockholder company. People from the sixteen villages could buy stock for $5 per share. They also looked for land and funding. The local land office was well organized, and Jack searched for land titles, buying only land with good coffee-growing characteristics.

It took several months, but Jack found several ten- to twelve-acre land parcels. Funding was available both from ICA and the Jamaican government, so residents began to purchase and plant coffee in the shade of larger forested areas already on the land.

This whole process took about a year. Once the legal organization was formed, title to land parcels secured, and coffee planting began, Jack found qualified leaders from within the communities as officers for the Blue Mountain Development Company (BMDC).

The officers sought and hired both a general manager and a coffee manager. Soon, all sixteen communities were involved, and BMDC had several hundred stockholders. All the officers were from the villages, and advisors came from the ICA Jamaica office. One of the early keys to success was a 240-acre piece of land owned by the Jamaican government lying fallow. With Jack's help, BMDC got the government to agree to give them rights to plant on the land, and this became the center of the project.

As the project developed and stockholders became more involved in planning and execution, the government and ICA decided to withdraw gradually and let the new company function on its own. Jack's last involvement was to hear that they had secured a letter of availability for occupancy and use of the land. With the organization in place and the shareholders doing the planning and management of the budding project, Jack felt his job was done. New horizons might exist elsewhere.

• • • • • •

Jack decided the next place to work was Haiti. He found out that Haiti had a variety of problems, not the least of which was hunger. He was encouraged by the PCUS, which had completed a merger agreement with the United Presbyterian Church (UPC) to combine into one large denomination. It was called the Presbyterian Church (USA) and was headquartered in Louisville, KY. David Young encouraged Jack to contact Hôpital Ste. Croix in Léogâne, Haiti. Their new denominational partner already had a history of involvement and it might be a good place to start.

Jack was pleased to discover that the First Presbyterian Church of New Bern had already visited Hôpital Ste. Croix and was eager to work on hunger in Haiti. In conversations with Louisville, the Presbyterian Church—now using the acronym PCUSA—and David Young decided the best approach would be to select one village. Theoretically, the village's progress in feeding itself would lead to broader acceptance of the program in other villages. It would make things simpler in the field (getting sixteen villages in Jamaica to agree had not been simple) and would fit the New Bern congregation nicely.

People in New Bern described it as partnering with a village. Jack remembered that people got used to saying, "We want to adopt a village—and we want to help a village—everything it takes to make a village go." Jack began working with Young in Atlanta, the local New Bern minister, and the American doctor who ran Hôpital Ste. Croix. He also sought anyone associated with development work and particularly with improved gardening techniques.

"Adopt a Village" became the popular phrase. Young and the doctor at Ste. Croix suggested they pick three villages to visit. Jack described it this way, "We found that there were little scatterings of land farmers, no one had much, and to help them might make a significant difference in their lives." Jack, Evelyn, and another woman from the church went to Haiti and visited the selected villages. One was on the plain between Léogâne and the nearby coast, one close into Léogâne, and one up a small river and in the mountain foothills.

By the time they got home, they had decided to adopt the mountain town. Poverty was more severe. People were more malnourished. With better gardening techniques, farmers would get more nutritious vegetables. Quickly there would be marked changes.

The name of the town was Bigonè, a collection of about six houses on a creek leading to the Cormier River. It was about two miles upstream from the main road running south from Léogâne. Bigonè had about fifty people living in the area, perhaps five or six families, including grandparents and many small children.

Most of the kids had reddish hair and potbellies, sure signs of malnutrition. It was the perfect community to adopt. Small enough, it was located in the lower mountain ranges and represented the most dramatic example of needed change.

Growing seasons in Haiti are short. Better methods and more nutritious vegetables would have an impact in short order. Perhaps the church could have the same kind of success in Haiti as they had in Jamaica!

Jack soon planned a second visit, this time with a gardening expert. They were excited that the villagers would quickly grasp the new concepts, and a new and successful project would be on its way. They chose dates, arranged for knowledgeable translators provided from Ste. Croix, and contacted the community. Everyone gathered in the village for what might prove to be an excellent start to working on hunger in Haiti.

The meeting was a complete disaster.

The whole town showed up. Families, small children, babies running around naked, older people frail and bent—all were there. Everyone sat outside in a shady area offered by the one tree at the edge of the creek. All the attendees were respectful and appeared to listen intently. They nodded in agreement as the gardener explained the new methods of planting. Better vegetables would not only provide adequate food but would also improve their health.

But when the meeting was over, no one asked questions. At all. The translators prodded and prodded, asking why no one had any questions. Weren't the new techniques good ones? *Yes.* Were the procedures clear, so they would know what to do? *Yes, they were clear. We know what to do.* Then tell us what you think of these ideas.

Finally, it appeared they had asked the right question. People shifted nervously, but at first none of them raised their hands, until finally a village elder said, "There is only one problem. We don't have any gardens.

The rains washed away all the soil years ago. The land here is only good for raising beans, and it is hard to get them to grow."

It turned out this was true of every village in the area, even those on the plains. The soil washed down the mountains, and on the plains, topsoil was buried by the subsoils that washed down. Incredibly, there were no real gardens in almost all of Léogâne, especially in the mountains.

Jack and the others already knew there was little forest vegetation left in Haiti; about 98% of the trees were already gone. Exploitation of forests from the outside was one problem. A government led by dictators for thirty years was another. A third reason was significant economic instability combined with an inefficient bureaucracy. Cutting trees for charcoal was the only source of income. This marked the end of any real chance for the forests.

Jack's significant visionary leap was that he realized they needed to work the whole watershed.

What a dilemma. But Jack and the others returned to New Bern with a new plan. Jack put it this way:

> We realized we'd have to help the whole watershed. As we left Haiti, we knew that supporting a village under these circumstances would be impossible. This is what brought us away from the idea of supporting a single village.
>
> We realized to make any significant impact it would have to become a watershed project. All communities were interconnected and totally dependent on the vagaries of the rainfall, which also meant flooding and little or no rain in the dry season.
>
> Bigonè is in the Cormier valley. We had to go back to New Bern and change the plan from a single village to an entire watershed. But obviously we had to enlist other churches since it was a much bigger project than we had envisioned. In Haiti, to get better in focus we needed to find the communities that were "leaders," so to speak.

Jack found out there was a planned government census in Léogâne county. The Presbyterian Church and the Episcopal Diocese of Haiti (EEH) jointly supported Hôpital Ste. Croix. They had worked with government health agents in Léogâne Commune (county) who conducted the census. Some agents worked in the Cormier valley. They were agreeable to adding some questions pertinent to agriculture.

Jack's group got valuable information about the distribution of farmers throughout the valley. And since the EEH supported development projects, they had money to hire a person to get additional information regarding agricultural practices. One of the tasks was to identify potential leaders. The person, Clemold Balezar, was sufficiently well known to be quite acceptable. Everyone called him Tinole (tee-noll).

Information gleaned from the census included how many were cash crop farmers and how many worked for others. Also, whether they owned or rented the land, or whether they were simply squatters who farmed the land. It was a pretty good indication of the economy of the valley.

An Episcopal priest named Père Racine headed up what Jack had begun to call the Cormier Development Project (CDP). Tinole participated, along with another new hire, Jean (Jn) Sémé Alexandre, who owned some property in Cormier and who lived in Carrefour (also called Kafou) close to Port-au-Prince. Jn Sémé was well respected and did a good job getting things set up and deciding how to proceed. Several churches in the states had committed to $10,000 each, so they had money to function.

By now there were several people involved in CDP. It made sense to form a committee to keep things moving along. The Episcopal diocese agreed and offered to have Père Racine head it up. There were several on the committee—Gerald Tismais, Carlo Napoleon, Tinole Balezar, Jn Louis Abner, and Jn Sémé. Some were priests and some farmers, and they met once each month. They met for two years but didn't accomplish much. It is important to note that the participating priests got a modest stipend for their effort, so continuing unproductive meetings was OK with them, even if not for the farmers.

After one rather raucous meeting late in the period, the committee decided they didn't know how to get started. They needed an experienced agriculture advisor. They wanted an *etranjè*, a foreigner. So they asked the hospital leadership and Jack if that could be arranged.

It now had been two years since the original meeting at Bigonè. Hope of duplicating the Jamaican success had now dimmed. The idea of adopting a watershed was fully formed and still believed to be a good one. Jack had raised some money; more was possible.

But not much had occurred in Haiti. People still starved, were still malnourished, and trees still were cut down to make charcoal to sell. And the rains still washed down into the valleys and flooded the plains, especially during hurricanes.

It was time to move forward. Finding a foreigner who was an agriculturist, an *agwonòme*, was the next step.

Chapter 3

Rodney Babe, the Designer

Jack went home and reached out again to David Young, who was now part of the combined Presbyterian denomination. The PCUSA opened a position search for a mission coworker to lead an agriculture/reforestation project in Léogâne with great promise. No one applied. Apparently the job was so unique, no one had the skills. After some months, Jack asked if he could help out since the church sources were a dead end.

Jack called other church denominations asking if they knew of mission-oriented people who might have the needed skills. One church had a facility in Port-au-Prince where many Americans visited to connect with other missionaries in Haiti. Jack contacted the person in charge, and they were helpful, recommending he contact a man named Rodney Babe.

They said Rodney had been living in Haiti a few years, spoke Kreyòl, and had prior agriculture experience. The best part was that he was considering changing his assignment so he could stay in Haiti.

Since Jack wasn't going back to Haiti for two months, he asked if Rodney could contact Dr. Richard McNeeley, a Presbyterian Church missionary who was the director of Hôpital Ste. Croix.* McNeeley was in tune with the plans for the agricultural project. When Jack recounted this for me, he said that after Rodney visited with the McNeeleys, "He ripened to the project and its possibilities." So Rodney applied and was found to be more than adequate. The PCUSA decided to call him to the position of Mission Coworker for the development project in the Cormier Valley.

For a complete history of Hôpital Ste. Croix in Léogâne, please visit this URL: http://www.emmf.com/hscroix.htm. Episcopal Medical Missions Foundation, 501 E. 32nd St., Austin, Texas 78705.

Haiti Fund (HFI) was thrilled to have found an agriculturalist. The PCUSA had broadened its mission work in Haiti. And the Episcopal Diocese now had someone who would bring progress to the fledgling Cormier Development Project. Everyone was happy.

But Rodney's reporting arrangements were complicated. Haiti Fund, Inc., would assume responsibility for funding the project work. The PCUSA agreed to pay the salary and benefits for Rodney. But his nonproject expenses would be paid through the Diocese of the Episcopal Church in Haiti (EEH) and reimbursed by the PCUSA to EEH. During the fifteen years of Rodney and (later) Sharyn's tenure at the Léogâne project, this somewhat convoluted organizational reporting structure never changed.

But the various people who were Rodney's physical bosses changed many times. Bishop Garnier retired, and a new bishop was elected. The newly elected bishop, the Right Reverend J. Zache Duracin, had been raised close to the project, so there was hope this would augur well for everyone, particularly Rodney. Bishop Duracin became Rodney's new Episcopal boss.

Jack Hanna later retired and was replaced short term by the executive vice president of HFI's board. Then Haiti Fund hired an individual to become Executive Director of Haiti Fund, reporting to the board. Rodney now had a new Haiti Fund boss. Finally, the new PCUSA after the merger made several changes in how they organized and directed the worldwide mission agency. This affected Rodney's reporting relationships in Louisville.

While such transition seems normal, the difference was that Rodney always had several different bosses *at the same time*. Never easy, it was even worse when working in a foreign country, with a foreign culture, and in a foreign language. Rodney defined, designed, and implemented the project under these bizarre conditions.

The PCUSA changed how it viewed the work of missionaries in the field by requiring them to spend more time in the States speaking to interested churches and presbyteries. During these times the denomination often held meetings for missionary rejuvenation where other missionaries could discuss common issues and problems.

In the early days, Rodney and Sharyn continued to live in Port-au-Prince, and Rodney went to Léogâne each week to get things moving in the right direction. Sharyn worked for Quisqueya Christian School in Port-au-Prince as a guidance counselor. This continued for a couple more years as Rodney focused on the project. The PCUSA rented a place in Léogâne for Rodney to live during the week, because the leg from Port-au-Prince to Léogâne could add more than two hours one way.

Because of Rodney's various reporting relationships, the focus of his work developed into four primary tasks:

- designing, determining, and implementing environmental restoration initiatives;
- carrying out health initiatives important to the mission of Hôpital Ste. Croix;
- providing an interim supply of clean water and food until the project provided them; and
- managing these first three while dealing with social, political, and cultural barriers and the hardships of day-to-day existence in Haiti.

Environmental Restoration

Restoring the environment was essentially an open book. Haiti had no established practices. The Haitian government had attempted reforestation programs many times. However, these were usually in response to natural disasters like hurricanes, but there was no measurable change.

During the time the Duvaliers were in charge of the government (Papa Doc 1957–1971; Baby Doc 1971–1986), leaders paid little attention to either the environment or rural needs. François Duvalier (Papa Doc) came to power during an amnesty period. He had served as minister of health prior to a coup in 1949 and went into exile until the amnesty in 1956 provided for democratic elections.

When elected, Duvalier moved quickly to consolidate his power. Steeve Coupeau points out this was not new: "The authoritarian culture is as old as Haiti itself."* Early in Duvalier's term the military moved to oust him, so he replaced top officers and then instituted the National Security Volunteer Militia (MVSN). This became known as the *Tonton*

Macoute—meaning bogeyman. Literally, *tonton* is uncle and *macoute* is a shoulder sack or bag. Small children are teased if they disobey by being told that their "uncle with a sack" will come and take them away.[†]

---

*This is one of many references on this particular period of Haiti's history. Steeve Coupeau, History of Haiti, (Greenwood Series of the Modern Nations), Greenwood Press, Westwood, CT, 2007, p. 93

†The first time I visited Haiti, I carried a backpack over my shoulder. We visited a school that had a small preschool with several children meeting outside. Some of us went outdoors to see the children. A small child saw me, a white man with a bag slung over my shoulder. He screamed loudly and promptly buried himself in the teacher's skirt, who was laughing and enjoying the moment. Later I learned the meaning of what had happened.

Also, during the Duvalier regimes the market economy gave way gradually to an economy that became more and more one of survival— essentially a subsistence economy. The elite in Haiti include the high-level government people and wealthy, educated families in Port-au-Prince and Cap Haitien. The distance between the elite and the rest of the population grew much larger under the Duvaliers.

In rural Haiti, this meant that family heads had to spend increasing amounts of time finding food (and often, shelter). This also drove the economy to become much more entrepreneurial, as the family head could not depend on anyone else for subsistence. It was like this when Haiti first became independent, and the entrepreneurial tradition continues today. There are many individual vendors along the streets and roads of Haiti, urban and rural, with plenty of buyers for food and other items for their families.

The meaning of this economic change in the rural areas was pronounced. It would not be wise, farmers reasoned, to try to collectivize and have large plantations. Besides, during the revolution at the end of the eighteenth century, all of the sugar plantations were abandoned or burned or both during the conflict. Later, many of the people fled into the mountains to avoid the invading French troops during Napoleon's rule. This system of *lakous* (small communities consisting of a few houses) has existed ever since.[‡]

‡*The most edifying discussion of this entire period is found in a recent history of Haiti by Dr. Laurent M. Dubois, Marcello Lotti Professor of Romance Studies and History and Co-Director, Franklin Humanities Center Haiti Laboratory at Duke University. Laurent DuBois,* Haiti: The Aftershocks of History, *Metropolitan Books, Henry Holt, LLC, 2012, New York, pp. 32–33.*

Also, by the mid–twentieth century the system of land tenure (ownership and occupancy) had been following the French system for 150 years.* Consequently, many estates were broken up and had a plethora of owners. The size of any given property segment subsequently grew smaller and smaller. Also, since many of the owners began to leave Haiti for more economic opportunity elsewhere, it was more difficult to sell parcels of land.

In England and many other European monarchies the system of inheritance was called primogeniture, where the oldest son inherited the entire estate when the landowner died. Hence, landed estates remained the same size with few owners for centuries. In some parts of France, however, siblings inherited an equal amount, so after many generations the number of people who owned the original estate could be extremely numerous.

The legal system required all owners to sign the documents, but this was rarely possible. Also, rights began to be conferred on the persons who were occupying the land. Today those persons using the land—farming it, erecting buildings on it, living on it—have rights nearly equal to landowners, especially respective to those who are absent from Haiti.

Therefore, at the beginning Rodney had to learn how to deal with the issues of land tenure. Gaining access to land to plant trees was a key to success. Leaders realized that erosion was the main contributor to the problem. They needed to plant on the hillsides, yet most of the hillsides were denuded completely of trees and soil by 1991.

So stopping further erosion in the mountains was the first step. The second was creating a way to reclaim nutrients in the soil. They attacked this problem on a variety of fronts—whether to buy seedlings for planting or germinate them locally, how to plant them to ensure at least

60% survival rate, and to find the locations to best retard erosion. And all this needed to be decided while solving the land tenure problem.

Many of the hills had lost so much soil and subsoil that their slopes were greater than 30% grade.[†] Peasants typically planted beans, cassava, sweet potatoes, and corn. But growing them was dicey, as crops washed away when large amounts of rain fell. Nutrients in the soil were so lacking that, if there was no rain for a while, the plants would die from the harsh sun.

---

†To put this grade in perspective, state roads with expected speeds of 60 mph in North Carolina have a 3% gradient as a maximum.

To determine the erosion rate, Rodney showed the groups how to take water flow measurements in the Cormier River. Bigonè (the original site chosen to improve gardening techniques) was one site measured. During the rainy season, it typically does not rain every day but every two or three days. When rains come, though, they can be substantial.

Water flow in the Cormier River during an "off" day by rough measure was calculated to be equivalent to one gallon per second, or 60 gallons per minute. Twelve hours following an inch-and-a-half rainfall one night, the flow at Bigonè was estimated to be 40,000 gallons per minute. Twenty-four hours later (no additional rain), it was still 180 GPM, three times the flow from the first day. Other measurements from time to time confirmed this flow rate.

And the water was a muddy brown color, obviously containing run-off from farther up the hill. The flow of brown water was a good demonstration for everyone, but the question was how to get the farmers to understand that this was caused by having no vegetation farther up the hill.[*] It was no wonder there were poor crop yields and much hunger.

During the spring of 2014, two graduate students in education from the City University of New York visited CODEP to conduct research for their master's thesis. Their theory was that learning is easiest when students participate rather than read the subject material or listen to lectures. To test their theory, they prepared a written text in Kreyòl to read to one group of Haitian farmers, and made posters which they used when speaking to a second group. But, they proved their hypothesis when they demonstrated the same material to a third group—showing the benefits of having vegetation to control erosion.

They used three 1.5-liter water bottles as containers, slicing through the empty bottles from top to bottom but leaving the bottle neck intact. They then filled each one with dirt. In one they left the dirt only, added grass in another, and added grass and small tree seedlings in the third. With a large audience of Haitian farmers watching, they poured water from the high end of each bottle and tilted each one at an angle so water would drain out the neck at the bottom of the incline. They drained the water into three clear plastic cups.

The first cup of runoff water was cloudy and brown, the second grayish in color, and the third clear—showing that reforestation was far superior. It was an instant hit, as all of the people wanted more bottles so they could replicate the experiment in their home lakous.

It was hard to get purchased seedlings to grow for a couple of reasons. The hot sun would make the seedlings so weak that a large percentage would die within the first month. Also, there was no guarantee that enriched soil was used when the seeds germinated, and this also could cause the plants to die.

Test containers to show the differences in runoff water color—using soil alone; soil, rocks, and grass; and soil, rocks, grass, and tree seedlings. The results were dramatic, and CODEP leaders insisted on keeping the containers to show their individual groups.

Gabion walls help shore up the Jacmel road against erosion.

Seeds germinated locally could be planted with compost and fertilizer. Watering them nearly every day with larger quantities of water the week before planting would help ensure survival.

It was equally important to prevent further erosion on the hillsides. Gabion walls were a good solution. These are weirs and dams made of bales or cages of rocks covered and secured on all sides by galvanized wire, using chain-link fencing. These could be lined up along the contour of the hills. A few meters farther down the hill, another section could be built. Placing dirt behind each row of bales filled in the gaps, and trees were planted in the spaces between.

Another method to prevent erosion was to dig long, shallow ditches along the contour of the hill and plant trees above them. Then leaves collected in the ditches and combined with moisture trapped in them to form a natural compost. Either of these methods worked, but each also required planting fast-growing stabilizing grasses that had deep root systems. Thus, all the hard work would pay off during the rainy season when the steep hillsides were most vulnerable to washouts. The preferred method for the past several years in the project has been the long-ditch method.

Choosing places to best retard erosion didn't happen scientifically; it was a matter of planting where land was available. Farmers who had access to land on behalf of their lakous were eager to try the new methods. Some plots were extremely steep—more than 30° grade—while others were less than 15°.

In almost all cases, however, farmers who were most eager to participate had lost crops—beans, peanuts, corn—due to heavy rains and were willing to try new techniques. Planting trees might not have been their first choice. But they soon learned that after three years, forest trees provided enough shade to support fruit trees and gardens, which were planted right in the ditches, where dead leaves and moisture collected in the ditch provided a natural compost to create nutrient-rich soil.

One particularly difficult problem was that free-range goats ate almost everything! Unless a particular lakou had enough people to stand guard, the goats could clear a newly planted plot in a few hours. Goats were everywhere in the mountains. So leaders sought a tree species that the goats wouldn't eat—one that made them sick or tasted bad, or that kept them away.

Rodney experimented with different varieties of trees to solve the problem. It turned out that eucalyptus trees (which are not native to Haiti but were introduced for erosion control in 1947) were the best choice. They are fast growing, strong smelling, have an acrid taste, coppice* naturally when cut, and are of little interest to the goats. For holding grasses, vetiver grass was a good choice because it is strong smelling, the roots in particular. Varieties of vetiver are used for making perfume.

Coppicing originally was a method of managing forests in England where trees were cut off at ground level and would regrow with many shoots from the original trunk. With the issues in Haiti of cutting trees for making charcoal, to have a naturally coppicing species makes them especially valuable from an erosion control perspective.

By this time, the new project was doing agricultural development in the Cormier River watershed. It was called the Cormier Development Project, or CDP. Jack discovered that it was hard for Haitians to "hear" the letters in the acronym CDP, so Rodney suggested they begin to call the project CODEP, for *Cormier Development Project*, which became the local name it carries to this day.

Health Initiatives

The PCUSA was Rodney's employer and, because it had ties to the Episcopal Diocese of Haiti through Hôpital Ste. Croix, it also had things for him to do. CODEP was uniquely qualified to carry out some health initiatives the hospital wanted.

The national health service in Haiti has community health workers who monitor trends and administer programs the government uses to improve the health of its citizens. Institutions like Hôpital Ste. Croix (HSC) have additional programs that supplement the government's efforts

Since hunger in rural areas is a constant threat, population control is one way to reduce the amount of foodstuffs needed for the local population. In 1978, HSC was chosen as a USAID test site for the implantation of Norplant contraceptive devices used for population control. These devices were developed as an effective implant to provide birth control for up to five years. Haiti was one of the test sites.

The process involved subdermal implantation of a series of six small* silicone capsules in the upper arm, and women generally needed no further monitoring. The procedure was cost effective, had long-term effects, and did not require extensive follow-up—all important factors in countries like Haiti. After five years, new implants could be changed when the old ones were removed. Implants contained slow-release progestin, a hormone used in birth control. CODEP implanted approximately 25% of the Norplant devices from HSC in the early 1990s.

---

* *The size of each capsule was 2.4 mm x 34 mm, or about the size of a matchstick, a tenth of an inch by one and a third inches. The capsules went in the upper arm and lasted for five years.*

Note: By present cultural sensibilities the use of contraceptive implants in developing countries around the world was manipulative and fraught with unresolved conflicts between their use and the lack of available medical follow-up. It is not the purpose here to weigh in on the ethics of these kinds of issues but simply to report the facts as I understand them.

It should be pointed out, however, that the FDA in the US approved the use of Norplant implants manufactured and sold by Wyeth Pharmaceuticals for general use in the USA. Given the population math for countries like Haiti and that women had little knowledge of birth control options—the culture precluded their having much decision-making authority—having too many babies to feed was a constant problem they faced.

Clean Water and Food

Rodney was tasked with supplying clean water and food in the interim until the CODEP project was self-sufficient. Most organizations label these two functions primary health and food security. Although broader than in the CODEP context, the reality was that the people living in the mountains were malnourished. Solving the problem meant relying on other NGOs (nongovernmental organizations). Four organizations were of particular help—OIM, FURREC, ADRA, and MEDA.

The **Organisation Internationale pour les Migrations (OIM)** was originally organized following World War II for the purpose of resettling displaced Europeans. Independent from governments, it was able to dispense advice and provide humanitarian assistance to ease the transitions many people faced. Founded in Vienna, it is currently headquartered in Geneva. For Haiti, OIM provided services and materials conducive to the establishment of democratic grassroots organizations.

For CODEP, OIM's assistance came in the form of materials to build a water catch basin with a large apron to provide a method of drying grain. Farmers could spread grain on the large concrete area, which doubled as a water catch basin during the rainy season. It was important to have dried foodstuffs stored for consumption at a later date. The water basin not only collects water for use for watering plants, animals, and for human consumption, but the saved water does not cause runoff erosion in the immediate area. Also, OIM constructed a large metal grain bin so secure storage could be utilized. Finally, OIM assisted with reforestation, providing tools, seedlings, buckets, plastic bags, and fertilizer.

Keeping the Haitian peasants interested in this work presented additional issues. Their whole lives were spent seeking food for their families; it was hard to have a planning horizon longer than a few days. The work of CODEP depended on farmers being able to focus on years, not days, into the future if sustainable development were to become a reality.

FURREC was a Canadian program that provided wages for specific work projects. FURREC is a French acronym for Civil Reconstruction and Emergency Fund. Over the course of the middle nineties, CODEP got two grants from FURREC, which provided daily wages through work projects. The people working in CODEP would not have to worry about a source of income during this period. Thus, they could focus on the long-term aspects of what they were doing.

The next problem for CODEP participants—and those not in the project—was water. An organization named the **Adventist Development & Relief Association (ADRA)** provided the solution. Capturing naturally occurring springs in the valley provided water both for agriculture and for human use, and this water was typically purer, meaning healthier.

ADRA also had programs related to food security. These included Food for Work, Food for Health, Food for Education, and School Feeding. If CODEP were to become a long-term reforestation project, having a ready source of food would be a necessity.* ADRA had a warehouse in Léogâne, so delivery of food from close by was possible.

Subsistence farmers think in the very short term: how will I feed my family Tuesday? Thus, if they don't have a food source, they'll cut down trees to make charcoal to sell to buy food. Having a food source would enable them to think of the long-term benefits of reforestation.

Rodney obtained several grants over a few years, and the result was that each family was able to get the equivalent of a bag of rice and a container of cooking oil sufficient to last a month. As a result, farmers had time to learn the techniques of farming so as to reclaim the environment, and the first step was reforestation.

The **Mennonite Economic Development Associates (MEDA)** played the last, and uniquely important, role by providing microcredit loans to farmers and roadside vendors who provided a bridge in areas that had no capital available. More about this program later.

Barriers to Project Design and Implementation

The difficulty of conditions simply cannot be emphasized enough as the project gained momentum. Because of Sharyn's employment in Port-au-Prince, Rodney had to drive the thirty miles to Léogâne, then head up the hill to project sites for discussions with the farmers representing the lakous. During times of political upheaval, travel time often could range up to four hours one way from Port-au-Prince to the project sites. Rodney had to take two trips to project sites each day to properly monitor progress. He also had to take potable water and food along each day. How to accomplish this in good humor was a test of the most laid-back personality.

There were seven CODEP groups initially, and the geographic distances (to say nothing of the elevations) between them were significant. PCUSA and HSC arranged for living quarters for Rodney in Léogâne, so he was able to spend several days in the project each week. Travel times improved, but transportation and communication were extreme as measured by current standards.

Electricity often worked only a few hours a day. Telephone service was erratic, and nonexistent in the mountains. Also, there was no electricity past Léogâne, so there was none in the project unless you had a portable generator. Cell phones didn't exist, and the Internet and email (both of which presume electricity and transmission towers or lines) were in their infancy. Skype and FaceTime didn't exist. Weather predictions were nonexistent or inaccurate, and law enforcement was often capricious and arbitrary.

Overlaying all this was government instability that is hard to imagine, even though Americans read about it at the time from news stories and broadcasts. Jean-Bertrand Aristide became the first democratically elected Haitian leader, inaugurated as president of Haiti in February 1991.

Seven months later, he was ousted in a military coup. During this time, the military leader, Joseph Raoul Cédras, who continued as the de facto leader of Haiti, ceded the presidency first to Joseph Nérette with elections planned for November. However, the US objected, Nérette resigned, and the chief justice of the Supreme Court, Émile Jonassaint, took his place as president.

This maneuvering caused the UN and the US to place an embargo on Haiti. As a result, many items were rationed, and it became increasingly hard for CODEP to get fuel and supplies. All gasoline and diesel were rationed, so travel became much more difficult. The ADRA warehouse in Léogâne had insufficient fuel to operate properly, and distant locations like CODEP were hit especially hard.

Other issues soon developed as shortages of all kinds became the norm. Planning by NGOs and other entities all suffered, as missionaries couldn't count on anything. The embargo lasted three years, although certain companies qualified to avoid the embargo on humanitarian directives issued by President George H. W. Bush and extended by President Bill Clinton. The government had taken power by force and showed no signs of moving toward free elections. A plan was made to invade Haiti by force (Operation Restore Democracy) to put Aristide back into power to serve out his term.*

---

*Journal of Haitian Studies, *Vol. 8, No. 2, 2002, p, 70 Philip R. Girard, Ohio University "Operation Restore Democracy?"*

But this plan was converted to a peacekeeping action (Operation Uphold Democracy) after former President Jimmy Carter, US Senator Sam Nunn, and General Colin Powell visited Cédras as the invading force neared Port-au-Prince. With the invasion force on the way, Cédras agreed to capitulate. Interestingly, he had been a student of Powell's at the Military School of the Americas some years earlier, which may have played an important role in saving what could have been much bloodshed.

During these times, managing the project was complicated even further because of all the political maneuverings. You can find abundant examples of this in the archives of Haiti Fund, Inc. For example, Rodney writes:

Work was greatly complicated by the OAS-UN embargo against Haiti. On an average, two days per week were lost by myself doing work in Port-au-Prince. With practically no telephone service, personal meetings with all collaborators were difficult to arrange. Cancellations were the rule as everyone was encountering similar problems.

Two major projects, requiring nearly a day per week included attempting to secure PAC-Humanitaire fuel for the pickup and preparing a major "food for work" proposal with ADRA. (Both were granted in early April 1994.) Purchasing supplies for cisterns and other needs was complicated by increasing unavailability and delivery problems.

Fuel problems necessitated frequent maintenance on the truck fuel filter system. Also, several hours weekly were wasted siphoning fuel from 55-gallon drums, transferring to jugs, and funneling into the truck. I stayed some nights at Hôpital Ste. Croix to conserve fuel rather than driving to Port-au-Prince.

Increasing poverty in the project area led many residents to request a food for work program. Many were already volunteering two days per week to do conservation work. On their request, I began in December contacting several large agencies.[†]

---

†*Haiti Fund, Inc., Unpublished Archives p. 61, (Quarterly Report by Rodney Babe, March 1994).*

What is most important to understand is that, through all this, Rodney continued conceiving and designing plans for fulfilling the agricultural needs of the project. Moreover, they were implemented successfully and effectively and, most importantly, began to work. A list of the things that had to be done is the best way to explain this early project success:

- food *had to be* provided so the farmers no longer needed to worry about their families;

- the way to dig contour canals *had to be* explained, understood, and then checked daily;
- preparation of nurseries and compost pits *had to be* conducted properly to assure success;
- methods for mixing soils, packing plastic bags for germination of seeds *had to be* demonstrated;
- using the proper techniques to side-dress with fertilizer at planting *had to be* demonstrated;
- proper treatment and secure storage of tools and materials *had to be* demonstrated so that the project's assets could be safe-guarded;
- setting goals and the importance of reaching them *had to be* stressed so project leaders could focus on performance; and
- honesty and integrity by all participants *had to be* pointed out and enforced in ways that gained cooperation, not revolt.

And, these goals were carried out in spite of the issues of merely trying to travel around Haiti in the midst of political, social, and cultural realities. The organizational reporting issues were never simple for Rodney. During this period he had to communicate constantly. Also, a variety of interested parties outside Haiti—agriculturalists, donors, and others—wanted to know about the new farming techniques.

Rodney developed and implemented project tasks into a culture that had never tried them. Since the people were completely inexperienced, Rodney constantly encouraged and gave them verbal support. Reporting authorities were complex, and misperceptions of the role and function of CODEP and its director had to be dealt with constantly.

There is no doubt all the participants, beneficiaries, and supporters (including me) of CODEP are deeply indebted to Rodney Babe for recognizing and creatively solving problems within the project, as well as remaining steadfast through many years of challenges external to the project. These contributions were essential to the increasing success of CODEP.

Chapter 4

Finding Haitian Leaders

When Rodney started, there were two Haitian leaders already on the payroll. Both signed on in the earlier stages of the project. One, Tinole Belezar, was hired to execute the agricultural survey as part of HSC's health census. But he apparently had rather meager credentials, was more interested in the health work than farming, and had not supported hiring Rodney. As a result, he soon left the project.

The other, Jn Sémé Alexandre, also had participated all along, plus he was one of the main advocates for finding *agwonòme* Rodney in the first place. He also owned land near where the project would start. He spoke Kreyòl, of course, but also French, as did Jack Hanna, so that would ease communications. The only drawback was that he lived in Kafou, a western suburb of Port-au-Prince, and travel to the project each day was arduous at best.

The project scope was the entire valley, and while planning was going on in Bigonè, the committee met with a family living in a higher elevation. Even before Rodney came, this family had volunteered to allow some of their lands for experimentation. Madame Kercelin, who lived in an area called DeLouch, on the Jacmel road, invited the committee to her home for discussions.

The Episcopal priest Père Racine led the conversations on whether a test plot should be started to determine if reforestation was possible. Madame Kercelin wanted to see whether the donation of some land for planting could finally get the project going.* However, Racine maintained that the focus should be on planting gardens and that reforestation was too costly, too long term, and gardens would solve the problem quicker and easier.

But, as priests' opinions carry considerable sway in Haiti, the meeting resolved nothing. Skeptics might wonder whether Père Racine, who received a stipend for each of the meetings, might have had an interest in prolonging the planning process rather than seeing the project get started. I am not sure, but in Haiti hidden agendas often can bar making real progress.

The astute reader knowledgeable in the cultural proclivities in Haiti might find it strange that a woman would take the initiative to offer land and welcome people to discuss it without her spouse present, especially in a patriarchal society like Haiti. The writer has found that women living in rural Haiti along the Jacmel road are particularly forceful behind the scenes. They will step forward to take charge, but only after a full vetting in private with their spouse and family first. The fact that the meeting came to naught must have been particularly disappointing since she must have spent a large amount of what I would call her cultural capital to set up this meeting.

When Rodney arrived, the search continued for a landowner living in the project who would donate land, a first effort in conducting reforestation. After many conversations they found an older woman who appeared to be perfect—her husband had recently died, she had considerable land (by Haitian standards), and had some nearby.

Madame Davide lived in an area a bit farther up the river from Bigonè in an area known as DeLouch. Also, her property was close to the Jacmel Road so access would be easier than across the other side of the valley. A meeting would be arranged to coincide with Jack Hanna's next visit to Haiti.

Jack, Rodney, Jn Sémé Alexandre, Edvy Durandice, and Krisne Naude all attended, as well as several local farmers. A most special guest was Bishop Garnier, the Episcopal Bishop of Haiti. The largest Episcopal Parish in the area, St. Etienne, was close to where the steep path led down to Madame Davide's. Since she spoke French, along with Jack, Jn Sémé, and the bishop, that was the preferred language, and nearly all the rest of those present could understand what was going on with French being spoken.*

---

* Today in rural Haiti, it is necessary for the etranjè to learn to speak and conduct all communications in Kreyòl. Twenty-five years ago this was not the case. Although all Haitians speak and understand Kreyòl, it was not adopted

as the second official language of Haiti until 1979 (the other being French). It is a French-based language, as is the case with Creole in Louisiana, Madagascar, and several other former French colonies. In Haiti, there are several other languages having influence, including Portuguese, Spanish, Taino, and West African. When it was adopted, however, it was determined that the orthography would use spellings that followed phonetic protocols.

Thus, for both the French and Kreyòl speaker, difficult written Kreyòl is understood easily if it is read aloud phonetically. Prior to the official determination that Haiti would have two official languages, all the schools taught only in French. Thus, older people in Haiti still today can communicate in French, while rural younger people strongly prefer Kreyòl. (A high percentage of younger people much prefer English as a second language rather than French.)

For more reading on this topic, see Jacques L. Bonenfant, Florida Memorial University, "History of Haitian-Creole: From Pidgin to Lingua Franca and English Influence on the Language," Review of Higher Education and Self-Learning (REHSL), Volume 4, June 2011, pp. 27–34.

Also, proper nouns in Kreyòl kept their French spellings, so you will notice throughout this book that most names are spelled using the French spellings and markings. The more notable names, however, commonly use both. An example is Léogâne (French), and Leyogàn (Kreyòl).

Madame Davide was both hospitable and enthusiastic. The team set the plan quickly. Jack had a sense that things would begin to move in the right direction from this point. "Madame Davide opted out of the field work because of her age, but she was the one who first offered her land for the planting of the trees, and she was central to the success of the project." Jack went home; Bishop Garnier went back to Port-au-Prince, and the project was off and running, this time with much brighter future prospects.

• • • • • •

It was important to involve participants early on and explain to them what the plan was so they would become enthusiastic supporters, so the CODEP team called a second meeting with a large number of people from several lakous participating. Approximately thirty-five people showed up and listened as Rodney and Jn Sémé explained what the concepts were and how they hoped to do significant reforestation over the next several years.

It would take three years' time for the trees to grow. Later, fruit trees, vegetables, and coffee would be planted. It would seem like a very long time, and they shouldn't cut down any trees. But, if they were patient, residents would see a remarkable change in the whole watershed.

Skepticism abounded. Residents asked questions such as: Why should we wait? Why does it take three years? What shall we do for food? Can we still plant three crops of beans? Won't the cyclones (hurricanes) wash away the trees, like they do our beans?

It was apparent the audience wasn't convinced yet. Rodney doubled down and explained many details of how many new techniques would make it possible. One superb inspiration was that he turned the questions around and began to ask them what they would do.

This technique had a triple purpose: It would give residents a chance to participate in the process of reaching decisions. It would give Rodney a chance to guide their thinking. And he could determine who among them had potential as leaders.

Rodney asked how they might plant seedlings so as to protect them. How do you keep the seedlings alive until you are ready to plant them? How do you ensure that you are planting the trees in a straight line and along the contour of the mountain? How do you keep them separated from one another so their roots won't grow together and risk killing them when you separate them prior to planting?

No one volunteered any answers. In Haiti, one never knows whether people are intimidated, being polite, truly unknowing, or simply feel uncomfortable conversing with *blans* (whites) in front of other local Haitians, even in Kreyòl. But the problem was so grave that everyone in attendance was willing to stay to hear the answers. One of the questions was posed again, reworded slightly to make it clearer. "Does anyone know how to lay out a line along a hillside that runs level, not uphill nor downhill?"

A long pause, then a hand went up. "You make an A-frame out of wood and use a plumb bob to walk it along the hill, putting stakes in at each level corner. Then follow the stakes." The man saying this was Madame Kercelin's son, Clement. Rodney explained that tree planting was relatively simple, once a level row was established. (Plant the seedling with a spade of earth pushed aside on the contour of the hill. And then mash it back in place with the seedling inserted along with a dollop of fertilizer and a small amount of water.)

Rodney and Jn Sémé asked other questions and again got no answers except from Clement, who knew a few things. But everyone's interest was piqued, and the stage was set for some learning to occur. But they chose to discuss only a few questions. Better to end before minds became saturated and began to wander.

After the meeting, Rodney sought out the young man who knew how to lay a level line in the mountains. "Where did you learn about laying a contour line?" Rodney asked.

"I worked on the docks in Port-au-Prince, and we had to make sure the containers were level when we stacked them. It was much flatter there, but I figured it must be the same technique in the mountains. Plus, for a short time, I worked for an NGO that was trying to get gardens to grow, and they used the same technique," the young man said.

Rodney invited Clement to begin working in the project and to learn the techniques. He had access to his mother's land and could begin to help set stakes marking level lines along the hillsides. Because he already knew some things, there was a chance he might become a leader.

Rodney needed leaders in the project, people who could take charge when it was difficult for him to get there every day. Jn Sémé was already onboard, and two or three other people had showed maturity and good sense during the first few weeks Rodney had become involved in the project.

One was Edvy Durandice. He lived farther up the mountain, in an area that represented another potential zone. T. J. Sanno, who lived in between Edvy and Clement, was also a possibility. There might be times when Jn Sémé might not be able to come all the way from Kafou, especially during the rainy season, so this group of three might be just what was needed.

In DeLouch was a family named Saintfleur, with a middle-aged woman named Elyseé, who also wanted to work. Madame Elyseé was signed up and showed leadership capability, if only because she was willing to take the step to ask to become involved. She was quiet, self-effacing, and a hard worker. Time would determine whether she would emerge as a leader in the male-dominated society.

It is interesting to note that the process of selecting initial leaders was an iterative process. People couldn't participate unless they had access to land. They represented the lakou where they lived. Much data needed to be reported to verify the best techniques, so potential leaders needed to be able to read and write. Finally, they needed to do the work in an organized manner using proper methods and monitoring progress.

Prime tasks involved buying seedlings to plant, keeping them alive until planting, and timing the planting periods to take advantage of rains. Eventually, this meant that tree seedlings were planted at the beginning and end of the rainy season (April and November) so that there would be an adequate supply of water to nurture them. Species planted needed to be hardy enough to survive the dry season from December till mid-April, yet not be overwhelmed with too much moisture during the rainy season.

Preparing the land for planting was the backbreaking labor involved. It was important to plant carefully along the contour to take maximum advantage of the water—either retaining it during the dry season or keeping it from eroding the planted areas during the rainy season. Farmers had long been accustomed to planting beans two or three times per year, typically in a line up the hill, but they experienced washouts regularly.

A washout was a significant threat to the family—a crop that washed away was devastating. Even those farmers who planted beans on the contour experienced washouts because they planted them too close together (wanting to maximize yield), and heavy rain would wash out the whole crop during a severe downpour.

It is hard for us to comprehend the perspective of the typical Haitian farmer during this period of the project. Because of political instability during the first four years of the project, access to food was more dependent than normal on the crops the individual family could grow. Rice and beans were the staples of the diet of nearly everyone in Haiti living in rural areas. Where possible, fruit trees provided mangos. Papayas, bananas, and plantains were also grown.

In most mountain areas, planting fruit trees wasn't possible, save the occasional mango tree. Bananas and plantains are shallow-rooted plants, and the failure rate is significantly higher than with other plants, as not only rain is a threat, but also strong winds that could flatten a crop. A few breadfruit trees grew, but their season was short. Farmers grew corn, but it was susceptible to pests, especially rats, after harvesting. Peanuts and potatoes (both regular and sweet potatoes) depended on good soil; even then yields were frequently poor.

A family's very existence was dependent on a variety of factors, any one of which could deal a death blow, literally. Imagine how difficult it must be to have to reduce the portions children in the family receive. Why children? Because they are too young to work. To save portion size, you add significant amounts of water to the bean sauce to make it go further, causing everyone to have reduced nutrition and thus, energy. Bad options, both.

Little rice is grown in Haiti for a variety of reasons, the main one being the government was no longer able to provide subsidies for farmers as before. Also, the severe slopes in the project area made it difficult to prepare rice paddies. Once again, land tenure was a huge issue, as few could gain access to a sufficiently large parcel of land to create a paddy because of ownership and land title issues.

The leaders of CODEP needed to learn all these things. Most importantly, they needed to have the leadership skills to impart that knowledge to others who worked in the project. Haiti has a long tradition of unmet expectations of government largesse—failures of vision and leadership, the definition of project scope and design, and a tendency on the part of the people to wait for government officials to act on behalf of the people.

This is incredulous to Americans, who prefer not using the government, because it is considered more inefficient. In Haiti, where the federal government is a bloated bureaucracy, counting on it to solve problems on schedule and within budget borders on fantasy. Still, the culture accepts the folly. Bear in mind, there is little anger or reproach; people accept that some are always ready to take advantage of a situation to their personal benefit.*

---

*As one can imagine, Americans find little patience to deal with these kinds of situations, whereas Haitians seem simply to accept them as part of life, and likely appreciate the spunk and initiative of those who are taking advantage of them.

So leadership gradually came to CODEP. But this did not mean that universal acceptance of the new concepts was quick or easy. Farmers still had to figure out a way to get food and water for their families every day, and obtaining it on a regular basis consumed them all the time. Jack Hanna believes that one of the things that helped a lot during this period of instability was that both the Canadian and US governments developed programs to help the Haitians obtain food.

In fact, Jack believed that the reasons for such programs was "that there were several religious organizations that benefitted from the US and Canada having guilty consciences concerning Haiti. They were distributing cooking oil and rice. The US and Canadian governments were funding these make-work projects to make amends for what they had done; not the best program for development work."

Among the government entities that were involved were USAID (United States Agency for International Development) and the CIDC (Canadian International Development Corporation). They helped private nongovernment entities carry out aid programs. The European Union also contributed. NGO programs were best because they had people and expertise. They left out the Haitian government because it was inefficient and unwieldy. It wasn't deliberate, but was certainly an acknowledgment of the realities of getting things accomplished on the ground in Haiti.

As noted before, ADRA, FURREC, and MEDA all were active in the CODEP area. Much of the success of these interim programs depended on providing short-term employment of needy citizens. FURREC and ADRA corporations instituted make-work projects, street sweeping, and road clearing.‡ The fledgling CODEP was able to use this largess to prepare land for reforestation. FURREC provided funding for people to work in the project. This was good, because in the sensibilities of the mountain people in the county, if the people in Leyogàn city received such aid, then CODEP people deserved it too.

---

‡*Interestingly enough, the same thing but from different organizations was done following the 2010 earthquake. Only now they call it Cash for Work—a way to get money into the economy following a disaster so the economy can get going again. But for CODEP, I was afraid it would become a huge problem. Cash for Work pays*

rates of $5.00 US dollars per day, and our stipends in 2010 totaled $3.75 per _week_, so we expected to lose a large number of our roughly six hundred people. But we did not lose any.

The reason apparently is that the Cash for Work jobs lasted only two weeks, and with the unemployment rate so high, it might be several months before an individual got hired again. CODEP was a reliable presence. That happened several times during the project—the Haitians realized that long-term involvement, and thus reliability, were important attributes for their lives. Whether this is anecdotal evidence of the culture moving away from its traditional subsistence perspective is doubtful, however.

ADRA was also one of the recipients of the money that began to flow from the US and Canada. ADRA HAITI became known in 1995 through an extension of its activities in several parts of the country with a five-year food program because of a grant of several million US dollars. As noted before, the name was linked to the "Food for Work" programs such as Food for Work . . . Health . . . Education, etc.

ADRA had a large storage facility near Léogâne, and rice was distributed to CODEP and other groups. ADRA's program implementation was made extremely complicated by poor management in Haiti that ultimately caused a crisis followed by a suspension of activities of this program in late 1999.* Or, as Jack cryptically put it, "After a few years, the 'conscience-salving' on the part of the US and Canada evaporated, and both the make-work money and the cooking oil and rice supplies stopped."

---

* Source: http://www.ADRAHaiti.org.ht/history.html.

MEDA began doing microcredit loans in the area. The regional representative was Jn Claude Cerin, who traveled to the area with some regularity and had twenty-two zones throughout Haiti, each with a separate loan administrator. Apparently local people had shown great interest in the process of applying for a loan because MEDA soon needed a local person to be the loan administrator.

The tasks included everything related to the applications: sorting them, determining recommendations about which applications should be approved, and then administering the money and collecting the repayments. All loans were for a six-month period and carried a 2 percent-per-month interest rate, an effective 24% annual interest rate. Borrowers paid most loans plus interest promptly. The system worked.

For the CODEP area, Rodney and Jack were pleased that the person chosen by Cerin was Edvy Durandice, one of the original workers in the project. They had recommended both Jn Sémé and Edvy for the position. Apparently, Cerin felt that Edvy, a local resident, was the better person for the job. He had good banking intuition and was well respected in all the communities along the road. Thus, he was someone whom the people trusted and, therefore, were pleased to ask about getting microcredit loans. His influence and leadership skills would continue to develop.

Edvy's cousin was also an intriguing person. Dures Durandice was a farmer, pastor, and school headmaster with a strong spiritual sense. His church was held each Sunday at the school that operated during the week. One might find him in beat-up gum boots, a soiled shirt, and shoddy old belted pants with a huge machete hanging at his side—looking every bit the peasant farmer.

Two hours later, he'd be in a white suit, immaculate tie, and ready to lead the school or stand in the pulpit to preach. His strong faith and leadership of a nondenominational church no doubt brought pastoral and theological comfort to the people whose lives were often simply too conflicting and complicated to manage alone. Dures could be counted on to provide a broader perspective and vision for CODEP as it moved forward.

Jn Sémé, Clement Kercelin, Edvy Durandice, and Pastor Dures were on board as leaders, and with Madame Elyseé showing promise. The organization was now universally known as the Cormier Development Project, CODEP. Leaders were leading, farmers had supplemental foodstuffs—rice and cooking oil—so they could concentrate on the longer term and the forests that would result.

The day-to-day issues of simply getting things to work in Haiti no doubt took its toll. In general, however, things progressed well. But there were many things to learn, and the learning curve was steep. But, before we turn to that, intriguing questions began to emerge: Just who were these new leaders? What were their personal stories? How could it be known whether they would have longevity as leaders?

Such stories are so important in a full understanding, not only of CODEP but also of how successful sustainable development works. Thus, as I indicated in the preface, I have chosen to highlight the lives of three of them, two inside CODEP and one living in the area but not a participant.

Chapter 5

Clement, the Salesman

Clement was finishing up his presentation to a group of about fifteen Americans who had stopped by to see the CODEP project one warm January day in 2015 in the mountains. They had gotten caught in traffic in driving out from Port-au-Prince. He knew that spending only two hours would not make it possible for them to really understand. Therefore, he broadly explained the complexity and magnificence of this twenty-four-year-old reforestation and sustainable agriculture development project.

Clement Tercelin coordinates all of the logistics for CODEP and provides tools, manure, compost, seeds, plastic bags, and a variety of needed things throughout the project. Full of nervous energy, he works harder than anyone I've ever known.

"After a few years, a Florida-based research company came and invited all the various agricultural projects in Haiti to a meeting in Aux Cayes." Clement spoke quickly in clipped Kreyòl sentences. He was standing on the edge of a steep precipice with thousands of mixed-age forest and fruit trees in the background. "They had a competition among them to see which one was the best. CODEP came out '*Numbe One.*'" This last part he said in his Leyogàn dialect, using the English words at the end.

As I translated for him (it is extremely powerful for the CODEP people to explain their lives and work to visiting groups), he looked directly into the eyes of several of them, smiling animatedly. He is the best salesman of CODEP concepts we have, everyone loves him, and his crackling personality shows through at all times. He even wants to be the guesthouse host of visiting groups one day. He doesn't speak English, but it is surprising how a few months of visitors who speak no Kreyòl will aid him in learning English.

How is it that Clement ended up doing this on that sunny day in January 2015? It began fifty years earlier with his birth on February 6, 1965. Hard into the Papa Doc Duvalier regime in Haiti, Clement's family lived just off the Jacmel Road in DeLouch. This is a section of Leyogàn Komin (county) located 550 meters (1,800 feet) above sea level. It looks out across the Cormier River Valley all the way to Leyogàn. As is typical in rural Haiti even today, he was born in his family's one-room house, his mother assisted by a midwife.*

I have lived and worked with Clement for most of the past ten years. The information contained in the stories about him come from several interviews recorded, some of his written notes, but also many long conversations as we drove to and from a variety of errands related to the project.

A healthy (and loud) baby would soon be bothering a younger sister. He was born into a mid-sixties divisive world with protests and anger—youngish people, restless and urging radical change, not only in Haiti but across the world, especially in the US. Lyndon Johnson was president of the US during the height of the cold war. François Duvalier had an iron grip on Haiti. Next door, the Dominican Republic was in the throes of post-Trujillo insurrections, riots, and a one-day civil war on April 24, 1965, when Clement was ten weeks old.

Daunting, to say the least. But Clement's effervescence showed through. It is hard to imagine the poverty and conditions under which rural farmers lived in those days. There was little money for food or clothing. All water had to be carried up from the river—a half-mile distance and some five hundred feet of vertical rise. Back up. Every day.

Many of the kids were red-headed with distended bellies, sure signs of malnutrition. Beans were the staple of the diet, and rice, when they could afford it, made the meal complete. No gardens would grow except in small, shady areas at the back of the house. There was no consistent side of the house with shade. Being located in a north-south orientation, the sun was always bright and intense. And in the three-and-a-half weeks before and after the summer solstice, the sun was on the north side of the house as it moved from the 18° of latitude to 23° before returning south about mid-July.

As Clement grew into a toddler and things stabilized a bit in the region, his father was able to get work in what is locally called "the Dominican." The pay was good, steady, and the work no-doubt backbreaking. Dad would return home about once a month, bring money, and the family would be able to eat, sparingly, until Dad came again. Clement was a bright boy, active, with many friends—cousins mostly—as they lived in a small lakou with four houses, and most people living there were family members.

Everyone was happy because Clement was *mawon* with tan-colored skin. He had a great-grandfather who was a *milot* (or mulatto) who had been born in Port-au-Prince.* It would mean great acceptance for the family—Clement was a blessed child. But times would continue to be hard.

Clement talks about Haiti recognizing four colors of Haitian people—nwa, mawon, wouj, and milot (black, brown/tan, red, and mulatto). Although these terms are offensive by present-day American standards and sensibilities, at least to Clement, they are real and useful. In our travels together, he will often point out someone who is wouj or milot. In the social system, particularly in Port-au-Prince businesses, one finds mulattoes heading the organization, with "red" secretaries (almost always female), and mawon and black workers at lower levels. This is not the case, as one might imagine, in government offices and at the airports and other places where a more egalitarian approach is common.

The tragedy, of course, is that in a land where unemployment is extremely high (running 60 to 85% in various locales) work often goes to the lighter-skinned people. It is hard for Americans to understand this without anger, and it certainly begs the question of what can be done to change it. I have lived in Haiti nearly six years, and it may be that resolution rests in the fact that it is largely generational. And the younger, more worldly wise and erudite Haitians will move away from what amounts to an effective, but subtle, caste system in Haiti.

Schools were plentiful, even in the mountains, but they were expensive and poor quality. Haiti has set high standards of education and has more than 15,200 elementary schools alone; approximately 90% are run privately by churches and NGOs operating from other countries, particularly the US.[†] About 90 percent of the children in Haiti are enrolled in elementary schools each year, attesting to the cultural predilection to educate their children.

---

†Schools not only in Haiti but in all slower-developing countries are one of the key opportunities for the future. Here is one source for Haiti's education system. "Education: Overview." United States Agency for International Development. 2007.

The system requires that all elementary students attend three cycles of three years each. This "fundamental education" tests each student before going to the next level. End-of-grade testing is at third, fifth, and ninth grades. (Recently, third-grade tests were suspended.) The government does the testing, and fees are paid beforehand. If a student fails, they have to wait until the next year, pay the fee again, and retake the test. Parents choose schools based on their percentage accomplishment on these national tests.[‡]

[‡] A more up-to-date reference and specific to Haiti can be found at *Suzata, Eriko. "Education in Haiti: An Overview of Trends, Issues, and Plans." World Innovative Summit for Education. (W.I.S.E.). Qatar. 2011.*

Since most of the schools are private, tuition costs vary depending on the location and the reputation of the school. Fees vary from about

$40 per year to as much as $100 for a student to attend. School uniforms, unique to each school, are not counted in this cost. Nor does it count the cost of taking the end-of-grade tests once every three years.

Technically, school is mandatory for all Haitian children between the ages of six and eleven. It is good this is not enforced, because in the CODEP area, children go to school only when the family can afford it. Often one child will have to wait out a year while a sibling has a chance to go "this year." As a further consequence, it is not uncommon to have a sixth grader who is fifteen years old or more.

It is important to understand that the culture places a high value on education, which means that school tuition and uniforms compete with other family needs, not the least of which are food and water. Our understanding in the US of these difficult choices is significantly limited, and we are prone to be blunt and ask why a child is not in school. This is embarrassing to the Haitian parent who doesn't want to plead poverty and who rarely even thinks in terms other than the harsh choices he is forced to make in such matters.

Such was the case with Clement, during an era when schools were much less ubiquitous and the standards were still low. His mother did not have enough money for him to start school until he was twelve years old, so by the time he finished the ninth grade, he was twenty! He was extremely fortunate because he could live with an uncle in Port-au-Prince who was an Episcopal priest, and there was a Seventh Day Adventist school nearby. Clement was able to go there his last three years.

In the mountains, secondary schools are much less common. There are fewer than 2,500 in all of Haiti, and approximately 80% are private. Half of the total secondary schools are in the Port-au-Prince department, Ouest (which includes Leyogàn).

To put this in perspective, there are sixteen leaders of CODEP as of 2015, and none has a high school *diplòm*, although four have a trade school certificate in agriculture. Further, there are three for whom basic literacy is a significant challenge. Should you assume this limits the project, it does not—they all have excellent basic intelligence, creativity, and well-honed social skills.

When Clement graduated from ninth grade in Port-au-Prince at age twenty, he was not sure what he wanted to do. He was a small, wiry bundle of athletic energy. He was an avid *foutbòl* fan, and a year after he graduated, Argentina won the World Cup with its star, Diego Maradona. Clement thought this was his future, so he began a regimen of training that was astounding.

His home was at KM 9 (and at 550 meters vertical elevation) on the Jacmel Road, and which went from Kafou Kolas to Jacmel on the South Coast of Haiti. It was 47 kilometers (30 miles) long beginning essentially at sea level with a vertical rise to 3,200 feet, just under 1,000 meters. From KM 9 to KM 27 at the top of the mountain was just over eleven miles, and represented a vertical elevation change of 450 meters, or 1,475 feet.

Not daunted by this in the least, Clement ran from his home to the top *and back* an average of three times per week! Athletes do this when training for a marathon, and Clement tossed it off as just a normal range of events. I used to run regularly, and doing five miles a day on level ground was quite the task. Granted, I was in my late thirties, while Clement was in his early twenties. Still, his feat remains awesome.

Restless and ready for new challenges, Clement decided to head back to Port-au-Prince and find his way in the world. This chapter of his life we take up later.

Chapter 6

The Steep Learning Curve to Success

At the end of chapter 4, I said that by the mid-nineties things were going relatively well in CODEP. There were still challenges, however, because of the culture, poverty, complexity of the organization, and new tasks and methods yet to be developed. This chapter shall deal with four of the challenges:

- keeping the farmers focused on the long-term project;
- being sure that techniques/methods were being followed while still making progress;
- continuing to develop leaders and move toward becoming sustainable; and
- assuring that land would continue to be available for planting.

There is no particular chronological order to this series of topics, but most of them took place between 1995 and 2000, at which time the project was moving toward maturity.

Keeping Farmers Focused on the Long-term Project

As noted earlier, ADRA and FURREC provided two valuable forms of assistance to CODEP during this period: vouchers to obtain food—rice and cooking oil—plus work-for-food programs that provided cash. Thus, CODEP participants were free to work in the project without worrying about feeding their families. However, both programs withdrew during this period, and the farmers took a double hit, as they had neither the money from FURREC nor ADRA's food. The threat was the loss of much of what had been accomplished since the project's inception.

The quickest, simplest, and most direct solution was to pay a stipend to each worker equivalent to the amount that ADRA had provided for food. It was a half-measure because the pay-for-work funds did not continue. However, since the main worry of the farmers was about feeding their families, this was the best way forward.

There is a strong caveat here, however, that went completely unnoticed at the time. Once you start a program like this, even if it replaces one that was intended to be only temporary, how do you bring it to a conclusion in an orderly manner? It is pretty easy to get used to monthly cash payments, and to stop the payments is likely to raise a hue and cry that could threaten the project. So, if the project is threatened unless you do something, it is likely *equally* threatened once you stop doing it.

To be sure, the stipend was small potatoes. Initially, it was fifty Haitian gourdes (HTG) per day. At mid-nineties exchange rates, it equaled $2.50 per day (USD), and $40 per month, working four days per week. This amount would buy enough rice and cooking oil for a month. However, farmers worked five days a week. All workers agreed to work one free day per week—a volunteer day—*jou volontè*. Thus, although working twenty to twenty-two days per month, the stipend represented pay for sixteen to eighteen days' work.

Everyone was happy, and project work continued apace. Later, work schedules were reduced to two days per week. Everyone gave one volunteer day, and the value of the Haitian gourde in US dollars fell to forty HTG to the dollar from twenty, a reduction in daily pay to $1.25. They raised the stipend to seventy-five HTG per day, but still the daily wage was $1.87 US.

At the time this was an elegant solution to a difficult problem. Viewed some fifteen years hence, it was a decision that would become very difficult to reverse. The Haitians, used to sudden changes in their lives, likely would have managed well. As the project grew and the number of participating communities increased, the costs for the stipend became a major cost factor in the project. Groups also soon figured out that if they had larger numbers of workers, there would be more people receiving the stipend. This was counterproductive to project goals and later on, we had considerable difficulty reducing and then eliminating the stipend.

CODEP experienced other issues in the early days as well: Trees were being cut down, and goats would eat the seedlings, both in the *pepinyès* (tree/seedling nurseries) and at the planting sites. After searching thoroughly it was found (as mentioned before) that both vetiver grass and eucalyptus seedlings were sufficiently strong smelling that the goats wouldn't eat them, so these became the preferred species for forest trees. In the meantime, workers would kill (and eat) free-range goats, so they provided an extra source of nutrition.

The system of charcoal manufacture, however, was so ingrained that trees were cut down to make charcoal, which ran counter to the purpose of reforestation in the first place.*

You may already know how charcoal is made. There are several ways. The method the writer has seen is to dig a shallow rectangular hole with a small lengthwise center ditch in it and line it with green, moist leaves. Blocks of wood are then piled on top, taking care not to block the ditch. Wood is placed inside, and the hole is filled to about 50% higher than the hole is deep, which is then covered with a thick layer of earth.

It is then lit by pushing combustibles through the center ditch and setting them on fire. Once the fire in the ditch is going well, everything is closed off and the entire thing allowed to smolder for several days, during which time the smoke that seeps from the earthen cover changes color gradually. It is opened after three or four days, the remaining fire quenched, and the partially burned small blocks of wood (now charcoal) put in large bags and toted to the nearest market for sale.

The big question was how to develop a system that would accomplish two objectives: provide a method for better control, and make provision for the trees to stay in the ground for several years. The incentive plan was born into the system this way, with specific goals established. A sophisticated point system was used to measure progress against goals. Goals included not only numbers of trees planted and the length of contour ditches (canals) dug, but also leaving the trees in the ground for specific periods of time. Thus, if a certain number of trees were planted and left in the ground for two years, the lakou would get a cistern.

Cisterns were huge time savers, and productivity improved in most lakous that had one because the women no longer had to trek to the creek or spring and back every day for water. During the rainy season, the five-hundred-gallon cistern would fill, and it would last for a long period during the dry season. Large-diameter PVC piping was used to capture roof rainwater runoff into the cistern. Close to the house, a cistern provided water that could be drawn easily for consumption, washing, and irrigation. What a joyful improvement in life.

In the late nineties, a builder working on the guesthouse at Lakil, Jack Stoner, became aware of the point system for cisterns and knew there was a need for a bigger, more valuable incentive, particularly since the cistern-qualification system, awarded after two years, only lengthened the horizon by that amount. A longer-term incentive would be an added benefit. Jack conceived a plan whereby skilled craftsmen from the US could come and build a large (by Haitian standards) house out of treated lumber. This obviated the need for concrete, which was especially hard to carry very far from the main road. Treated wood was resistant to termites and other pests, and thus was an additional incentive.

Thus, Jack's incentive gwo kay (large house) was an instant hit, particularly at long distances from the road. And the visiting carpenters were enthralled to live with a family for a few days to construct a house. All the lakou needed to do in advance was to level an area large enough to build the house, and then assist the carpenters in bringing tools, tents, wood, and galvanized roofing to the site. It took 513 points accumulated over about five years to earn a gwo kay; it became the ultimate incentive prize and a successful attempt at extending the focus from two years to five years.

Following Correct Techniques while Making Progress

Even as the incentives started, an amazing inconsistency still existed among the working groups. As noted earlier, twelve people served on the steering committee headed by Père Racine. When they voted to ask for an agwonòme to come, the vote was seven yeas and five nays. For reasons unclear to me, Père Racine was one of those in the negative.

Père Racine and the others soon left the committee. Those remaining had access to land, so they began learning the techniques and doing the variety of tasks Rodney assigned once he was on board. Soon there were six groups, each headed by an individual who lived in the area, and all of the plantings were on plots of land in DeLouch. Jn

Sémé didn't have a group because he was primarily Rodney's assistant since Rodney was not able to make the trip from Port-au-Prince to the project every day.

Once the incentives were in place, it is legitimate to ask: Would such a program of incentives become the main focus of the work? Would it extend the period before the Haitians took over the project themselves (not unlike the "teach to test" system in our schools today)? Jack Hanna felt that Edvy was a key to making the system of incentives work. But the answer would depend on the leaders of the six groups and how they stood the test.

At this point, CODEP had been in operation for several years and was making good progress. The culture of leadership had been very direct. Jn Sémé would visit the project several times a week and keep records on who worked what days. The group leaders were now holding monthly meetings. Prior to the meetings, Jn Sémé and Rodney would meet to share notes. When Rodney visited individual work sites, he could see where people were slacking and not following the agreed-upon procedures.

Often, particularly after Sharyn and he had moved closer to Leyogàn, Rodney was able to visit the project early in the morning. Then he accomplished other tasks during the day and then revisited either at the end of the day* or first thing the following morning. This helped ensure compliance with the methods and techniques of germinating, growing, watering, and planting seedlings.

The typical workday is roughly from seven a.m. to one thirty p.m. with no breaks except for coffee, when it is available. It varies by a half hour or so, but the end of the day for Haitians occurs before the afternoon heat becomes too oppressive. Contrast this with American visitors who sleep late and don't get to the project site until ten a.m. or so. They often find themselves hiking back to the road, which is usually in an uphill direction, in the middle of the hottest part of the afternoon.

Haitians nearly always will collect, by the way, wherever there is shade when they are talking or waiting for something. Americans, on the other hand, especially in winter, will stand in the sun, rarely moving to the shade until they realize they are sweating profusely. No wonder Haitians consider us crazy for some of our practices!

New Growth. These trees are about three years old, planted in a remote area with contour canals and vetiver grass to help stabilize the hillside. These trees will mature in another two years, and gardens, fruit trees, and coffee can be planted under them, providing shade so as not to be harmed by the harsh sun during the dry season.

Land preparation also was specific once a standard approach was developed. Early on, large, shallow holes were dug along the contour as a place to hold water and provide a place to add leaves and other materials to do composting. Then, when the seedlings grew to five or six meters in height, there was sufficient shade to allow more delicate plants to survive the hot sun.

Eventually, however, digging a ditch along a whole contour section was more efficient and worked just as well. Leaves of the deciduous trees accumulated in the ditches, and natural composting occurred along the ditch. It was a welcome change because by now the trees already planted were so numerous that it was not possible to continue composting. Instead, the compost was mixed with dirt and packed in plastic bags for seed germination. They called it "breaking dirt."

Still, the number of local groups continued to grow in fits and starts. At one time in 1996, there were over thirty groups. But once the groups understood what the work was and what land was available, many of the groups decided they did not want to participate. There may be many reasons for this, but among them certainly is the notion of how the culture viewed the work standards set for the project.

Rules were specific about methods and techniques, use of tools and maintaining them, and work protocols. In Haiti, when wages or food are part of any program, as many people as possible try to find ways to participate. This can border on the absurd. For example, when scheduled meetings occur, attendance often depends more on whether there will be food than the topic covered.

Also, there is a tendency for a few Haitians to think they can get away with stealing tools and selling them. While this may be common in Leyogàn and Port-au-Prince, in the mountains along the Jacmel road, population density is much lower. Family ties are close; the suspect is almost always found out.

One case happened where several wheelbarrows disappeared from CODEP stock. Everyone knew who had done it, and the wheelbarrows appeared one by one in the market in Kafou Dufort. The culprit was Krisne Naude, one of the original founders of CODEP. Rodney fired him for breaking the rules. This was good. Other participants learned a big lesson about discipline and that standards would remain high. Poaching would defeat the purpose of the entire project.

Developing Leaders and Becoming Sustainable

After five years, then, most elements of CODEP were moving along well. Earlier it had been necessary to purchase most of the tree seedlings planted from an NGO called Double Harvest. Now CODEP was able to harvest seeds, dry them, germinate them in plastic bags in pepinyès, and gain momentum in that manner.

School support was going well, with three elementary schools working together to teach CODEP principles. They even had small nurseries where seedlings could be grown and planted. The lakou groups were stable, and tree plantings and contour canals dug were goal-driven and predictable.

Following the dismissal of Krisne Naude, other leaders began to take charge more and more. Jn Sémé and Edvy Durandice attended an agricultural seminar in Hinche (north of Port-au-Prince) conducted by the World Neighbors Organization on project evaluation.

The people who were leading the effort under Rodney included Jn Sémé, Jn Claude Barthelemy, Clement Kercelin, and Dures and Edvy Durandice (who were cousins). Wensy D'Andreville was assisting with school support and taught at Pastor Dures's school at Siloe.

Several younger people were showing signs of developing into leaders—Berton Kercelin (Clement's cousin), Madame Elyseé, Bastien Aimè, Madame Enese, and René Decimé. It would be a few more years before they would reach that status, but there were positive signs.

The Episcopal Diocese of Haiti ran an agricultural trade school in the north of Haiti called St. Barnabas, located at Terre Rouge (red land). CODEP sponsored several scholarships for people to attend. They learned garden planting and land management but also some reforestation. Graduates received a certificate as an agwonòme.

Each CODEP leader had responsibilities related to the lakou groups they worked. They received other tasks on the basis of acquired skills. They technically were "hosting" the people who were doing the work, advising them, getting them energized, and helping them accomplish the work in an ordered manner. Rodney called them animators. The word *animatè* in French means to animate, in English to energize, and in Kreyòl to host. Therefore, using the word animator for these CODEP leaders is both a title and a description of what they do.

As the first few years passed, the geography continued to grow, even if the number of lakou groups did not. The reason for this is that the lakou often had access to several parcels of property and thus, when they completed planting one small parcel, they would move to another one nearby. They also learned about the simple logistics of the process.

When workers construct a pepinyè, it has a compost hole for making compost from dirt and manure and other organic refuse brought to the site. It will also have space for germinating and growing seedlings in plastic bags, and a covering framework structure that uses banana leaves to provide shade for the tender, newly germinated seeds. It requires many buckets to water the seedlings daily. Interestingly, the planting season is short—two or three weeks—so the main burden is to carry the water to the pepinyè for the four- to six-month period before planting.

As a result, groups soon learned to put the pepinyès relatively close to the source of water rather than where they would eventually plant the seedlings. They now knew that they would have to transport seedlings a longer distance at planting time, but only once!

Each animator had additional tasks of one kind or another that occupied him or her with other things each week. For example, Dures Durandice (Pastè Dures) had both a school that he headed as well as a nondenominational church that met in the school. Jn Sémé had properties elsewhere that he managed.

Clement Tercelin,* who had a driver's license, assisted with logistics—getting and delivering tools, fertilizer, and seedlings. Introducing new species required purchasing seedlings until there were enough trees of the new species to use their seeds for germination. And, as one might suspect, there was a lot of running around needed with such a geographically diverse set of working groups.

Because of a clerical error when his national ID card was reissued, Tercelin's official surname changed from Kercelin to Tercelin. He had to get his wife's and two boys' last names officially changed as well!

To maintain a sense of coordinated effort and monitor activities, the group of animators met on a regular basis, typically once or twice per month. At these meetings, they were asked to report on what they had accomplished, describe any problems, listen and learn from each other, and get guidance from Rodney Babe.

Thus, the animators learned to appreciate Rodney's brilliance as a creative project designer and agriculturist, who could take almost any problem and resolve it with a few pointed suggestions that worked well in practice. It was no small feat—as Rodney suffered a long-standing injury from a traffic accident that kept him from walking long distances. He was unable to visit most sections of the project. So any teaching and descriptions of what to do were described verbally. *And in Kreyòl.* Then the animators carried them out in the field.

Pastor Dures was another animator who developed additional techniques and showed a significant entrepreneurial spirit. He had rented several small tracts of land across the Jacmel road from the Cormier Watershed. He built terraces, planted gardens under the spreading shade of the trees, culled out forest trees as the fruit trees grew and expanded in size, and captured a small creek to irrigate along his gently sloping valley.

Many of the people working in CODEP lived in an area called Fonde Boudin, which was a completely different watershed. They had a chance to capture three additional small springs, which would solve the issues of water for the seedlings and for the families to drink. So, with little foofaraw, CODEP moved into its second watershed.

Also, Jn Sémé, by late in the decade, had realized there was a large area of land that was completely barren of trees in the northern sectors where CODEP was working. It started in an area on the right bank of the Cormier River, called La Ferrier. Two sections lower down were already participating, Bwa Gauche (left branch) and Gran Savanne. You can see La Ferrier easily from the Jacmel road, and it was on the main path from that road to Gwo Mon, the large mountain area behind. If land became available, La Ferrier would be a perfect spot to demonstrate the benefits of reforestation.

By the end of CODEP's first decade, it had established animator leaders, a few who had washed out, and others who were coming along. And expectations were high that the current leaders would be able to take increasing leadership roles as the project grew. It would depend on whether CODEP had access to land going forward.

Dealing with Land Availability

As noted, a constant issue was gaining access to land. Following Haiti's independence, the system of inheritance (particularly of land) became a significant issue, as the primogeniture method of inheritance used in England and other kingdoms in Europe was replaced with the one adopted in France.*

As noted before, several European countries based estate inheritance on primogeniture. The eldest son received the entire estate. It allowed continuous ownership of property and kept estates large and single families strong. One of the spoils of war was awarding property owned by the landed gentry to loyal knights.

In Langedoc in Southern France, it was done differently—they divided property equally among all the children. Therefore, typically there were forty or fifty co-seigneurs in the middle ages. As an aside, the Fourth Crusade, started by Pope Innocent, took place against supposed heretics in this same area. Not having sufficient lands to award as bounty for his knights is sighted as the reason Raymond of Toulouse lost the battles against the Pope's armies. For more, see Langedoc Property Inheritance Law. Source: http://www.midi-france.info/0814_inheritance.htm.

It all changed with Raymond's defeat, but the hangover from this perceived injustice continued until the French Revolution, which went back to the original Langedoc system of equal inheritance. Today in France, it is not possible to leave all your property to whomever you want. And in Haiti, much of the same principles apply. The degree to which this affects the huge issue of land tenure in Haiti is not known.

The strife of living in Haiti has created what Haitians refer to as the Eleventh Department, or the diaspora, consisting of all the Haitians who have fled Haiti, which is nearly one-sixth of the domestic population. It totals between one and a half to two million people in the US, Canada, other Caribbean Islands, and Europe.[†] Also, traveling in Haiti is hard, people living within the borders typically don't travel, and the system of residence addresses is not at all clear. Therefore, people are hard to find.

[†]*"Haiti." The World Factbook. Central Intelligence Agency, 2011. Note: the 2011 numbers differ significantly from those of 2010, which were influenced strongly by the demographic effect of the January 2010 earthquake; these latest figures more closely correspond to those of 2009.*

The combination of access to land and the legal system surrounding its use causes significant problems throughout Haiti. When purchasing a plot of land, the legal system requires that all the shared owners of the property sign the deed of transfer. After two hundred years, you can imagine that an original estate might now have many owners, perhaps hundreds. And with the diaspora of Haitians living all over the world, getting all of them to sign off on a sale is extremely difficult.

A concurrent development involved the increasing rights of the people who stayed and occupied the property as the number of owners multiplied. The legal system now began to provide more and more rights to the people who lived on the land and worked it.[*] Within forty years following independence in 1804, much of the plantation land was divided up consistent with that being practiced in France. This is still the case today, and both the rights of the several owners of a parcel of land and the persons who live on it are fairly clear in the law.

Richard A. Haggerty, ed. Haiti: A Country Study. *Washington: GPO for the Library of Congress, 1989, Land Tenure and Land Policy.*

It is certainly not efficient, but the stakes are clear. You can be a landowner and live on it and have relatively more rights than other owners who are not there. Or, you can occupy land for many years and accumulate rights whether or not you own it. Improvements to the property (such as a house) revert to the owner if you leave it. But the owner must compensate you for the original costs (not current market value) of any improvements.

A third way to gain land is to rent the property from the owner or owners. A rental agreement does not need to have all owners sign it, as it is not a property transfer. Often the owner is not the occupier, and if the occupier wishes to rent it, a contract is drawn up for a specific period and rent is paid up front. Rent costs are low, certainly compared to the purchase of the land. In the case of a land occupant, apparently the issues are not much different, but it is wise to determine the history of the occupant to be sure.†

---

†*Jacob Kushner,* "Who Owns What in Haiti?" *The New Yorker, January 28, 2015. For a different perspective on the issue of renting land in Haiti and the difficulties associated with it, Mr. Kushner's article is excellent.*

The land in La Ferrier was available. I mentioned it earlier. It could be rented for ten years. The total amount of land was about twenty-two acres, it had a south-facing exposure, and it could be seen from several spots along the Jacmel road. Also, the main footpath across the Cormier Valley to the next section of Leyogàn, Gwo Mon, ran right through the middle of the twenty-two-acre plot.* (This was the same footpath Debbie and I would take in 2006.)

‡*There are disputed accounts of exactly how much land was available, and estimates vary from twenty-two acres to forty. I will use twenty-two, with your understanding that it may be wrong.*

So, CODEP rented this plot of land. We will come back to this fascinating property later.

It became known as the demonstration forest, or La Ferrier, or both. Jn Sémé was active there because it was the closest spot in CODEP to his home in Kafou. Pastor Dures also took a keen interest because he wanted to start a school nearby. And, assurances of the rental contract were solid because Edvy Durandice had become involved. Because of his experience with MEDA, his skill set was something the project needed. The leaders were taking leadership roles. It made a big difference.

Chapter 7

Edvy, the Banker

Edvy tells the story this way: "We were standing together facing a wall in a very large room. All of a sudden the wall opened up and there was another small room inside. We stepped inside and the wall closed behind us. We stood there awhile and then the wall opened up again, and we stepped out into another, completely different very large room."* Do you recognize he was describing his first elevator ride? It was in the Cape Fear Valley Medical Center in Wilmington, NC. If it was like a typical hospital elevator, it was slow enough that Edvy didn't know he was ascending. Our daily experiences in the US and Canada become part of us. Thus, we often fail to realize that a common occurrence for us, such as an elevator ride, must have been a nearly out-of-body experience for Edvy.

Joseph Edvy Durandice. These notes are part of a series of conversations with Edvy over the period of the past six years, including the transcriptions of recorded personal interviews, beginning 7/20/14.

It was March 1997, and CODEP had been operating for six years. By this time, Edvy was already an animator and had also been appointed as a MEDA associate where he qualified people for microloans.

A few months earlier, he had noticed a lump on the back of his neck. After a visit to Hôpital Ste. Croix to see an American doctor, he was tentatively diagnosed with Hodgkin's disease. If left untreated, life expectancy for this type of cancer is as little as two years. Upon Rodney's recommendation, Haiti Fund decided to send Edvy to the US for treatment. He was a leader in the project, and it was important to get an exact diagnosis, receive the best treatment, and hope for a good prognosis. It seemed to be a good plan, particularly since this type of cancer is treatable with a reasonable expectation of complete cure.

How did Edvy get to this stage? Why hadn't he noticed the tumor earlier? Why hadn't he done anything about it? All valid questions except for the fact he lives in Haiti. In rural Haiti, there is little medication for pain, much less sophisticated medications for cancer. I haven't found where they did the biopsy and whether they sent the sample to the US for analysis, or if they did it in Port-au-Prince where laboratory analysis might be available. Edvy likely noticed the tumor but knew there was nothing to do about it. Such is the system.

The approach to and outlook on life in rural Haiti is very different than we are used to. People are stoic, like Madame Jacques, and accept what happens to them with a great amount of religious faith and acceptance of what life deals. We, on the other hand, fall apart if the "check engine" light comes on. In Haiti, when you are leaving and say, "We'll see you again," the response is: "*Si Dye vle.*" If God wants (it).

Edvy was born in his home in the Duklo section of Leyogàn on July 30, 1951. He lived in several places and went to organized schools for six years. He started in an area about five miles from where he lives and works now, and attended primary school for three years, beginning when he was eight years old.

He transferred to the national school at Parizon nearby, but it turned out to have low academic standards. Edvy was fortunate because his family found three tutors who gave the equivalent of an extra three years of schooling. The tutors took turns coming to his house, and essentially he was home-schooled at the end. He finished by the time he was seventeen. He wanted to go on to get a *filosof* degree, the equivalent of a high school education, but never did because he was already working two jobs.

At age seventeen, he found a trade school in Leyogàn that was teaching people how to tailor clothes. So he took the short course, learned how to make men's shirts and pants, and then invested in a treadle sewing machine.

He set up the machine in his home and began to make clothes on a per-piece basis at age nineteen. His skill was apparently high because he spent twenty-seven years as a haberdasher. He also hired four people to work for him to keep up with the orders in the pipeline. He did this work while continuing to farm—planting vegetables, keeping a few goats, and doing the best he could without much soil in the mountains.

Here is how Edvy put it to me: "I began to work as a farmer, and after that I worked to make clothes. I learned how to do it in Léogâne, and I worked a lot making different kinds of clothes—shirts, pants, vests, coats. I began doing clothes, tailor-made, and I did it by myself for almost twelve years. It was good work. Then I stopped making clothes and got four people who helped me. So with the help, I was able to make more clothes. I did it for people who paid me on a piecework business. There were a lot of people who did this."

Bear in mind that this period is what some call the heyday of clothing manufacturing in Haiti. During the regime of Baby Doc Duvalier, there was a push to increase several sectors of manufacturing, especially the garment sector. Many stories tell of the oppressive conditions in the small shops in Port-au-Prince* in those days.

For a more detailed accounting of this segment of the Haitian economy, see Roseline Ng, Cheong-Lum, Leslie Jermyn, Haiti; p. 40–41.

Apparently the situation in Leyogàn was quite different. They did the sewing on a per-piece basis, taking orders for delivery ahead of time, and most of the sewing was done in the homes rather than a factory setting. Although Edvy never got rich doing this, it is apparent that his entrepreneurial spirit was well-honed at that point in his young life. He had enough business that he needed to hire people to do part of the work.

Edvy was forty years old when the Cormier Development Project began, but his clothing business continued for a few years. When he was invited to become a loan officer for MEDA, he gradually gave up his clothing business because he no longer had time to manage it properly. Since he had access to land, he was one of the early CODEP leaders, along with Rodney and Jn Sémé. He often participated in the discussions on managing the project. He led a work group that continues today.

Since Edvy lived farther up the hill than any of the work groups, his group was able to do things a little differently. For example, Edvy's land had a couple of springs on it, so existing trees were available to act as a shelter for the tender seedlings. It meant that management of sunlight was more difficult; some seedlings needed relatively more sun and others less.

It wasn't long before others noticed Edvy's style and easy manner. He soon had more groups to manage. "Soon after that, I worked as an animator and had seven groups. This was after a year and a half. The work was in the higher areas of Kormier where the springs were, one in Parizon, two in Duklo, one in Bwa Gauche, one in Grand Savanne."

It was about this same time that the Canadian International Development Authority (CIDA) was set up to funnel funds into Haiti following Jn Bertrand Aristide's reinstallation to power. The private Canadian organization chosen to implement the programs was MEDA (Mennonite Economic Development Associates). They searched for ways to fund projects in rural Haiti.

The country director, Jn Claude Cerin, (mentioned earlier) was Haitian and had worked for USAID. He worked to establish a network of people around Haiti to be local representatives to find worthy projects and preapprove them for funding, subject to final approval in Port-au-Prince. Knowing of CODEP and Rodney Babe's involvement with it, Cerin asked Rodney, who recommended Edvy and Jn Sémé as possible candidates. Edvy described it to me this way:

"After I had worked for a while for CODEP as an animator, then Rodney needed someone to work for MEDA, and I was the one. It was a microcredit organization that assisted people and groups who wanted to have a garden. So, it also helped people get tools for making ramps and pépinyes* and also purchasing animals. MEDA began in 1993 or 1994, and I began working for them then, but I don't remember very well."

---

*Contour canals and tree seedling nurseries.

"It was a project which asked Rodney to provide the name of a person who could work for MEDA. He said Jn Sémé or I could do it. MEDA had money; they needed someone to help decide who would qualify for the credit. At first, I didn't think I had the right experience, but Rodney talked to Jn Claude Cerin, who was OK with me being the one. He was the boss and was a Haitian, who had worked for USAID in their credit program. He already had an agwonòme named Manno doing work elsewhere."

Rodney had gotten a separate grant for some funding for micro-credit, so they decided to put that into MEDA so the funding would have good tracking. Edvy continued, "MEDA worked in Cormier for about six years. Finally, the program of MEDA was stopped because the USAID money was stopped. It was a contract that didn't get funded again when it finished. Plus, the amount of money that CODEP had loaned the organization was too small to continue the program because MEDA covered various parts of Haiti. It was too expensive.

"There were several employees, they had vehicles, and the money that CODEP had put in paralleled the money for our area, but MEDA was a much larger organization. When they decided to close it, Cerin told us our portion would be about $30,000 US. We put half of it into the local Fonkoze bank at the top of the mountain overlooking the Cormier watershed.

"But, I told Agwonòme Rodney that it would not be possible to distribute the rest fairly among the CODEP lakous. Worse, people would not believe that it had been fairly distributed. So, the remaining CODEP share of about $15,000 was set up to build a building that could continue microcredit."

Note that I have included these extensive quotes to demonstrate that Edvy has not only a phenomenal memory but also a good sense of the big picture. This is exceedingly rare among people whose lives have, by necessity, been focused exclusively in the short term. More of Edvy's fascinating life will unfold later in the book.

Chapter 8

Responding to Donor Interest

A few years into the project, supporters who believed in the concepts that Jack and Evelyn Hanna espoused wanted to see the project for themselves. Although Rodney faithfully wrote regular reports with a wide distribution, the supporting church members wanted to visit, particularly since the political situation had eased somewhat.

It meant that someone needed to host groups and show them the project. They could stay at the Hôpital Ste. Croix guesthouse, about ten miles from the project. So this naturally fell to Rodney and now Sharyn, who had left her position at Quisqueya Christian School and could help Rodney manage the American visitors. But it was an additional job to do.

Groups began coming down to visit. Fitting them into the Hôpital Ste. Croix (HSC) guesthouse schedule was complicated. The first groups came for a variety of reasons, often combining a visit to HSC and seeing CODEP as part of the trip. The guesthouse was on the property of HSC, so CODEP wasn't far.

The balance between managing a mission and hosting donors to the mission is always a dilemma. Any mission project has a way of always needing your full attention, especially in Haiti. But making time for donors is absolutely necessary and must be managed as well. There are a variety of considerations:

- the kind of project it is, and how the donor views it;
- the distance from home to the project and whether the travel costs to the project outweigh the amount of money that would otherwise go to the project;
- support for a missionary, without regard to the project the missionary is working on;

- support for a specific project, without specific involvement with the missionary; and
- support of a hybrid nature, where both the missionary and the project are supported.

Each consideration is important, but the most important is the type of project. Also, some missions are based on having visitors, particularly if they have skills not available in the mission location. Medical missions are an example, where the skills and techniques are typically not available in the country where the mission occurs. This is the case in rural Haiti.

Also, a group's skills can be scheduled to achieve the maximum benefits when worked out in advance. As this is being written, the writer received an email from a pediatric surgeon in Los Angeles who is coming to Haiti a couple of months hence. Dr. Suzanne Yoder, who comes to Haiti twice a year indicates that she "will be bringing a pediatric general surgery team to Jacmel, Haiti this November. We will be working with the Community Coalition for Haiti space in downtown Jacmel (Jacmel portal Léogâne rue Bel Combe) from November 14th to the 20th. On Saturday and Sunday (11/14–15), we will be conducting half-day clinic evaluations of patients. Operations will be taking place from November 16–19th.

"If further evaluations are necessary during our operating days, we will be happy to see any patients. If you know of any patients with pediatric general surgical needs including but not limited to the following . . . we would be happy to see them in November. We also have connections to other surgical and non-surgical specialists and charitable organizations, so if there are other pediatric health issues you have questions about, we will do our best to connect you with the most appropriate provider."*

---

*Dr. Suzanne Yoder, unsolicited email to me on August 10, 2015. I first met Dr. Yoder on a flight to Haiti and found out about her work. Two of our animators' children had medical issues requiring pediatric surgery, and Dr. Yoder has been very helpful to get those scheduled and taken care of.

Other kinds of specialized mission trips include skilled craftsmen, agriculture specialists, education specialists, and work projects—and there are *tons* of the latter. To fully understand CODEP, it is necessary to view these various kinds of missions independent from CODEP. There are two major aspects to consider—relief versus development, and donor inspection trip needs.

Relief versus Development

We tend to describe mission projects as being in one of two categories: relief or development. Relief, of course, is in response to a significant and immediate need. This is usually a result of a natural disaster—hurricane, earthquake, tsunami, fire, or a health epidemic resulting from any one of them. Relief can be further subdivided into the specific kinds of relief administered: food, housing, water, medical, security, etc.

The definition of development can be broad. 1) *real property development*, 2) *economic development* (starting businesses and building factories), or 3) *conducting agriculture projects* (from gardens to farms to reforestation to forms of protein foodstuffs like fish, peanuts, or marketable projects like cocoa or coffee).

So categorizing any project into either relief or development often doesn't help a donor to know enough about the project to which she or he wants to contribute. People give to situations (often in response to a terrible natural disaster). They give to specific needs (an orphanage, school, or specific building requirement—housing, water well, school materials, etc.). And they give to ideas or notions such as solar ovens for baking without electricity or use of fossil fuels, environmentally friendly equipment like biofuels manufacture, and reforestation for flood control.

Defining exactly what a contribution means is sometimes hard. For example, it is a well-known belief that Americans are generous. You have heard people say that studies show that our response to disasters and even normal charitable giving is a much higher percentage than elsewhere in the world where data is available. However, it may surprise you that *this is not necessarily true*. Some statistics might help put this into perspective:

- In 2012, Americans gave a total of $316.23 billion, or just under 2 % of US GDP of $15.163 trillion.
- Of this amount, 72%, or $228.93 billion, came from individuals.

- Corporations, foundations, and estate bequests gave, respectively, 6%, 15%, and 7% of this total.*
- The Gallup organization annually compiles a World Giving Index which collects responses to questions about financial giving, volunteering for charitable work, and helping out strangers.†
- In reviewing the methodology of the survey, it appears not to be comparable to rankings of financial-only giving by country.‡

However, while the US typically is at the top of the World Giving Index compared to other countries, in 2013 it ranked thirteenth of all nations in making financial contributions.ˣ

The first three bullets above come from the National Center for Charitable Statistics, Household Giving as a Percentage of Total Giving. Source: Giving USA 2013: The Annual Report on Philanthropy for the Year 2012 (Chicago: Giving USA Foundation, 2013), p. 12.

† *philanthropynews.alliancemagazine.org/2013-world-giving-index-shows-potential-of-charitable-giving-in-emerging-economies/ (port 80).*

‡ *https://brainthing.wordpress.com/2010/11/29/world-giving-index-methodology.*

ˣ*Holly Hall, "Americans Rank 13th in Charitable Giving Among Countries Around the World", The Chronicle of Philanthropy, December 23, 2013, Washington, DC.*

When taken together, the willingness to contribute, to volunteer, and to help strangers in need is a strong cultural tendency among Americans. This is hardly news to us, as it confirms what we already believed—that Americans are leaders worldwide in responding to charitable needs. Americans are generous of their time and are always willing to help.

In fact, one of the issues CODEP struggles with is the notion of how we solve problems. Americans are known all over the world as problem solvers. They find a situation, analyze it quickly, often with few facts or data, define an elegant solution, work quickly to implement the solution, and then go on to the next problem.

When solving problems in Haiti, however, Americans are surprised to learn later that their solution has not been followed and implemented by the Haitians after they leave. Why? Because it is much more important in Haiti to establish relationships and socialize than to attend to deadlines, goals, or completion dates. Once Americans realize this tendency, they typically adapt quickly and devise solutions that accommodate these Haitian tendencies.

But still, the sense of helping and volunteering is strong. For example, hundreds of young Americans descended on Léogâne after the 2010 earthquake to find ways to help out. How this impacted Haiti is germane to the discussion of the issue about relief versus development. One of the best descriptions of this situation comes from a book called *Toxic Charity* by Robert D. Lupton. He states the case rather bluntly, far better than I can:

> Public service has moved beyond mere catchphrase or school requirement in our country. It is now a way of life for Americans of all ages. Nearly every church, business, and organization gets involved in some sort of service project. College spring break service projects and church mission trips have become the norm. Corporations realize they can enhance their images through cause-related marketing while also building up employee loyalty and pride in the company. The compassion industry is almost universally accepted as a virtuous and constructive enterprise.
>
> But what's so surprising is that its outcomes are almost entirely unexamined . . . Yet, those closest to the ground—on the receiving end of this outpouring of generosity—quietly admit that it may be hurting more than helping. How? Destroying personal initiative. When we do for those in need what they have the capacity to do for themselves, we disempower them.*

Robert D. Lupton, Toxic Charity: How Churches and Charities Hurt Those They Help (And How to Reverse It). *Harper Collins, New York. 2011. pp. 2, 3.*

Understanding about this tendency is improving. During the recovery work in Léogâne following the earthquake, weekly meetings would be held on various functional responsibilities—housing, food, medical, cash for work. Once every two weeks, the leaders would gather for a general meeting to discuss the overall effort. At one point, in discussing continuing aid, a UN official (from Africa) took the podium and stated flatly, "Whatever you do, please don't do to Haiti what was done to Africa—make her dependent on aid to survive." (Although I was not present to hear this statement, at least three people who were there related this story to me, so I do not doubt its veracity.)

Managing Donor Inspection Trip Needs

So CODEP, which had started with a failed meeting in Bigonè, was now to the point where thousands of trees had been germinated, grown, and then planted in the Cormier watershed, and it was now attracting interest. Donors wanted to see what this notion of sustainable agricultural development was all about.

The other factors noted at the beginning of this chapter were in sync: Haiti Fund, Inc. was raising money for the project itself, and the PCUSA paid the Babes' salary and administration costs. Haiti was near the US, so excessive transportation costs were not an issue. Missionary versus mission was defined: HFI existed to fund CODEP. Others paid the Babes' living and travel costs. And the Episcopal bishop administered things. CODEP was a hybrid project (mission, missionary, and a combination), and the organizational lines were clear. How this fared in the longer term was yet to be discovered.

But now it made sense to try to construct a separate facility for CODEP visitors only. Jack had an interesting way of putting it: "During the time of Bishop Garnier, he was very collaborative, and we would never have been able to do things without him. He retired and died and Duracin was named the new bishop. In those days, we were very optimistic, and so I said, 'Let's build a facility just for CODEP visitors.' We did parallel fund-raising for the project and the new building and were successful in both."

Two things happened concurrently—funding the guesthouse and searching for suitable land to build it on. Neither the PCUSA nor Haiti Fund could own property in Haiti, since only those organizations having specific legal status in Haiti and those individuals either holding a Haitian passport or a valid residence permit (*permis sejours*) could buy land.

No one knew how much money it would take to fund the guest-house, but everyone was optimistic that they could raise the needed amount without a lot of effort. By now there were at least fifty churches that were committed and participated with their support. A call was put out to the churches for people who had specialized skills who could be called upon to assist with the project—design, building, craftsmanship. Many people responded, so things were underway.

The preferred site would be near the project, could house Rodney and Sharyn, and could provide a guesthouse for visitors. Also, people should be able to live together without undue closeness. It was important to give the missionaries their space yet provide the guests ample room to relax and enjoy their visit. These needs led to some basic influencing factors on the design:

- The missionary quarters should not be attached to the guest-house but contiguous with enough separation to make everyone comfortable.
- The facility should be close to the project.
- The facility should be secure, so visitors and missionaries would be safe.
- Since many of the donors were likely to come to CODEP on a first mission trip, it should meet their US sensibilities for shared space, and yet allow them to become CODEP enthusiasts.
- The site must be accessible to the main roads in Haiti (through Léogâne to Jacmel on the south coast) so it would be easy to get to/from the airport in Port-au-Prince.
- It should be at least an acre in size to make the facilities comfortably spaced.
- Finally, the facility, wherever it was, must be able to be completely self-sufficient—water, power, gas, telephone, and another new concept in communications—Internet access.

You can tell these design-influencing factors were heavily influenced by the experience during the first six years of the project. During this time, insurrections, blockades, supply of materials and services, travel difficulties, and personal safety were huge issues.

In conversations with possible providers of land, the best opportunity rested with the Episcopal Diocese, which already owned many parcels of land in Haiti. Bishop Duracin assisted by involving several of his people who knew the properties that the church owned, almost all of them attached to one of several Episcopal parishes located in and around Léogâne and over toward Jacmel.

Jack Hanna put it this way: "We looked at lots of pieces of land, but there are no property records, and so it wasn't easy. The earmark was our optimism, which led to the contract we have between the Haiti Fund, Inc. and the EEH, signed by the bishop of the diocese, Duracin, and me."

Fortunately, there was a section at the site of Legliz Epifanè (L'Eglise Epiphane) in a place near Lakil (L'Acul) on the national road. It was about four miles past where the national road intersected with the extension to Jacmel. Its area was about two-thirds of an acre, somewhat smaller than desired. But it bordered the coast and was in a nice spot that met the rest of the established criteria. It was called Episcopal Beach since Episcopal priests often swam there.

The process of completing the agreement on the property and the construction project were the next steps. But first, let's go back to our story of Edvy.

Chapter 9

Edvy's Challenge

In chapter 7 I talked about Edvy's need to get treatment for Hodgkin's disease. We pick up the story a few months before his first experience riding the hospital elevator in Wilmington, NC.

As Edvy was washing his neck one morning, he felt a bump on it. Pushing on it caused no pain; it was just a soft, funny bump. He'd let it go and see if it changed in size. He went on his way, working with local farmers, helping them fill out their forms for MEDA loans, and being sure they were correctly written. This was often extremely difficult since most of them could neither read or write.

He would counsel them, asking why they should be considered a good risk for a substantial loan, at least by Haitian standards. A typical loan was $50 (US), and the interest fees were high—24% per annum repayable in six months with a 2% per month interest charge. So, $56 repaid a $50 loan after six months. In terms of Haitian Gourdes, based on the exchange rate at the time, the amounts were 1,000 HTG with the repayment amount of 1,120.

Edvy worked closely with anyone who wanted to qualify. Few people defaulted; accordingly they could get another loan at a different time. Those who did default couldn't get further loans, which proved to be an important lesson for all the participating communities to learn.

After a month, the tumor had grown. Edvy told Rodney Babe about it. Rodney insisted he see the next US doctors who came to Hôpital Ste. Croix. In January, some doctors were coming from Wilmington, NC, so Edvy got his chance to see them. Dr. Bob Jones was on the trip, and the reaction was swift and blunt: Edvy had cancer, probably Hodgkin's disease, a lymphatic system cancer that can spread quickly. A biopsy confirmed this.

This cancer in the United States was eminently treatable, but in Haiti there was practically no chance that it could even be treated, much less cured. Edvy was such a valuable employee, a leader, not only in CODEP but also in many of the mountain communities since he was a loan officer for MEDA; everyone knew and trusted him.

Edvy's illness was a real issue for the board of directors of Haiti Fund, Inc. Rodney Babe had been involved with CODEP for about six years, and Haiti was beginning to get back to normal. (Bear in mind, "normal" for Haiti is still difficult.) The programs with MEDA, FURREC, and ADRA allowed the farmers to focus on long-term agriculture, and the Babes were beginning to make a difference. The project simply could not afford to lose a leader like Edvy at such a critical time in its movement forward.

The above paragraph may seem crass and lacking in compassion for Edvy, like his health was a cold business decision. Few written documents address this situation, but people who were there say there was great compassion for what Edvy was going through.*

---

* Bob and Becky Jones, Jim Sylivant, Russell Thienpont, and others helped Edvy through this period in the United States. They all have fond memories of those days and how calm and reserved Edvy was throughout his stay in the US.

Edvy headed to Wilmington to start what would end up being six months of chemotherapy, radiation, and a strict dietary regimen that would result in completely curing him of Hodgkin's lymphoma. As you read this, you may think that a period like this would be one of uncertainty, boredom, and tediousness. Perhaps that is what would happen to any of us.

However, for Edvy it was a time for reflection, relaxation, and work. He asked Becky if she could get some dry goods for him so he could sew. He spent many warm afternoons on the deck outside his room at the Joneses sewing pants, shirts, and odd pieces of clothing, reaching back to his younger days as a haberdasher in Leyogàn.

Jim Sylivant, a long-time board member and frequent visitor to Haiti, wrote down his thoughts after Edvy first arrived in Raleigh, NC, on his way to Wilmington, NC, for treatment:

Edvy is forty-five years old, has a wife and five children, and owns a farm. He has become one of the people on whom Rodney Babe relies. The continuation of the community development of this region is very dependent on Edvy.

Edvy discovered a lump on his neck several months ago and brought it to Rodney's attention. Rodney arranged for him to be seen by a US physician from Wilmington, NC, who happened to be visiting Ste. Croix Hospital at the time. The preliminary diagnosis was Hodgkin's disease, later confirmed by a biopsy. Unfortunately, no treatment for this disease is available in Haiti, and without intervention, life expectancy is only approximately two years.

After much discussion by the board of directors of the Haiti Fund and many others who were involved, a decision was made that the best course of action would be to bring Edvy to the US for further evaluation and treatment. Many difficult obstacles had to be overcome. A passport and visa had to be obtained and arrangements made for his transportation, lodging, and medical care. Following a Herculean effort by many people to arrange for this, the date for Edvy's departure arrived.

Edvy speaks and writes two languages, Haitian Creole, and French, but not English. He lives in the mountains of the Cormier Region of Haiti in a small house with no water or electricity. The nearest electricity is 12–15 miles away in the seacoast town of Léogâne. It is difficult, if not impossible, for most Americans to imagine how he must feel or what he must think about the future.

We jump in our car and think nothing of running over to another part of town 12–15 miles away. For Edvy, getting to Léogâne means getting up before sunrise and waiting beside the only road that leads to the coast for a *Tap-Tap* (a truck serving as a bus) to come by. The fare is about 25 cents. Cheap, you think. Not from Edvy's point of view. The most money people in that region can expect to handle in a year is approximately $400.00. Compared to someone in the

US who makes $30,000 a year, that would be equivalent to $18.75 for a bus ride, so it is not something one often does.

When March 8 arrived, the day he was to leave his family and farm, he got up at 4:30 a.m., said good-bye, and took the *Tap-Tap* to Léogâne where Rodney and Sharyn met him in the CODEP truck. They left Léogâne for the airport in Port-au-Prince at 8:00 a.m. because, although the airport is only 30 miles and the plane was not due to depart until 3:00 p.m., it is not unusual for the trip to take three or four hours.

Traffic on the only road to Port-au-Prince is heavy and often only a single lane. A breakdown of a bus or truck can tie up traffic for hours. Sharyn dropped Edvy and Rodney at the airport and made her way back home. The plane carrying Rodney and Edvy stopped in Miami where they changed to a plane bound for the Raleigh-Durham Airport.

I was waiting at Gate 25 for them at 9:45 p.m. as they finally emerged from the plane. Edvy appeared no worse for the experience. In fact, according to Rodney, the plane ride was silky smooth compared to their ride to Port-au-Prince. We waited for their luggage to come around on Carousel B while Carol waited outside in our van. Edvy wore sandals and no coat because he had just come from a place where winter in March is typically 90 degrees.

Edvy does not own or need a winter coat. In anticipation of his trip, the Crestwood Presbyterian Church group sent him some winter clothes and other items he would need. The drive back to our house took only 15 minutes and soon they were sitting down to a late meal of soup after which they were ready for bed.

I took Edvy on a tour of his bedroom and bathroom and had to explain everything. I showed him the overhead light switch, but when I cut it off, the automatic night-light plugged into the wall outlet came on. I had to show him how it worked by covering and uncovering its photocell with my hand. He tested it several times himself by waving his hand in front of it.

Edvy Durandice. Edvy and "Junior," his grandson. Edvy has a large family with several grandchildren. He lives among them with two daughters and a son residing close by. On trips to the states, he invariably loads a suitcase full of toys to take home.

Next was the bathroom. I showed and explained how to work the one-knob lavatory, turning it to the right for cold and to the left for hot. Before showing him, I explained the principle and warned him to be careful not to get burned by the hot water. So as I turned it on, he tested the water but it was cold instead of hot. I then had to explain how the hot water heater was located in another part of the house, and we had to wait for it to make its way through the pipes.

We waited and waited. Finally, it turned warm, then hot. I was afraid he would get burned if he didn't understand just how hot it could get so after it ran for a while; I had him test it with his finger. Next came the shower, even more complicated with its one knob plus the plunger to transfer the water flow from the tub to the shower. He seemed to catch on, so I finished by explaining the toilet and its flush lever.

Rodney disappeared to his room, and soon Edvy emerged from his room and went to the bathroom to try out the shower. It ran for fifteen minutes, so I think he caught on and thoroughly enjoyed rinsing off the day's dust.*

---

*James W. Sylivant, unpublished article dated March 10, 1997, describing the overnight visit by Rodney Babe and Edvy Durandice when Edvy was on his way to Wilmington for treatment. Jim lived in France for two years and spoke fluent French, a great help to Edvy's first visit to the US.

All still marvel at Edvy's quiet demeanor, good manners, and graciousness during six months of his stay, in the midst of being beset by worries about his health and family. He did all this while speaking no English and in a consumer society where everyone and everything around him was new, somewhat strange, and completely different from his life in Haiti.

For Americans accustomed to having our leisure activities well planned and scheduled tightly in our otherwise busy schedules, we would be content with our Kindles, iPads, and paperbacks. For Edvy, though, this was something new. Not speaking English meant he had no particular interest in watching television. Not reading either French or Kreyòl very well (assuming you could find books in Kreyòl) meant that avenue was essentially unavailable too.

Also, telephoning his family in Haiti was nearly impossible in those days. The exception was when Rodney Babe, who had returned to Haiti, would call him on their satellite phone (meaning the conversations necessarily had to be kept short). So, Edvy sewed and sewed, and no doubt worried about his family, his condition, and the microcredit loans of his Haitian clients who also would worry.

Raised a Catholic in the area called Duklo (deek-lo), this was the first time Edvy had been absent from either Haiti or his family in his entire life. Born in 1951, one of four brothers and three sisters, Edvy was raised by a bean farmer father who had a most difficult time feeding his large family. They had (for Haiti) a lot of land holdings in small parcels, so there was always a lot of work to do.

As of this writing, two of Edvy's brothers have died, and the other is a Catholic priest in Venezuela. It is likely that one of the brothers died of cancer (in Hôpital Ste. Croix) while the other, according to Edvy, died from Vodou.* It may have been dysentery, but Edvy and many others talk about deaths from voodoo when the exact cause of death is unknown.

In Haiti, the term mystik represents a broad series of mystical, social, semireligious activities carried on by people in various parts of the Leyogàn county. The city is well known throughout Haiti for its rara celebrations. These are all-night-long marches (with bands, drums, sticks, and plenty of the local liquor, called Klarin) which are a bastardized version recreating Christ's journey to Golgotha. Most of the time, raras are held during the Lenten season; sometimes they are not.

The animators talk about families who die off from mystik causes, with no rhyme or reason. One of the animators, Madame Elyseé, has had a long history of health problems, including diabetes, high blood pressure, and extreme variations in weight. During the ten years I have known her, she (a large woman) has gone from 130 pounds to 200 pounds and back.

Three of her siblings have succumbed to mystik, and she has had medical issues. She even has spent a week on two occasions in Port-au-Prince for diagnosis, to no avail. So, she has been expecting to die now for two years without an apparent change in her condition. Makes you wonder at the power of suggestion inherent in such a belief system.

For more extensive reading on this topic, I suggest reading materials written by Elizabeth A. McAlister, Associate Professor of Religion and Theology, Wesleyan University, Middletown, CT, who wrote, Rara! Vodou, Power, and Performance in Haiti and its Diaspora, *University of California Press, 2002.*

After approximately six months, the tumor had receded completely, and further tests showed the cancer was in remission. So Edvy returned to Haiti, no doubt entirely ready to go home to his wife, family, farm, and microcredit work. Of course, this had been a new and unique situation for his wife and the entire family, as well as for the entire Duklo community.

In the last five-plus years, there has been little improvement in the services provided by the government regarding healthcare and disease prevention in rural Haiti. Government health workers are paid to survey the population and administer certain medications. There are few pain management medicines, and the medications available tend to be salves and ointments.

As a result, people who have pain are typically stoic in their approach to being a victim. Life is like that, and life deals harshly with some people. As a result, when foreigners (*etranjè yo*) come to do medical clinics, there are always large crowds.

This is surprising to the clinicians, who quickly adapt and typically triage the patients into two or three categories: those who seem to be fit but who need vitamins and deworming pills; those who can be treated for minor illnesses such as scabies; and those who need more attention and perhaps prescription medication, which the clinicians typically bring with them.

Canadian and American doctors often are frustrated that they cannot perform other modes of treatment such as minor surgery and other outpatient services common in both the US and Canada. But, from the perspective of the Haitian patients, the clinicians are God-sent people who they believe can (and do) make profound differences in their lives.

The prescription drug and over-the-counter meds can become a problem, however. This is one of the differences in culture that can make for misunderstandings that can never be known ahead of time. For example, almost all children need vitamins. In the US, children's vitamins are ubiquitous and can be bought at any drugstore or chain retailer. These sweetened vitamins are often the types medical groups bring to Haiti. Many clinicians now know they absolutely must tell parents that they should give only one pill per day to their child. Otherwise, Haitian kids will think they are candy and eat them all at one sitting!

Another cultural difference is the (mistaken) belief that any pill, regardless of its intended use, can help with any malady a particular person may have. I talked in the first chapter about the vendors selling pills at the Port-au-Prince airport. In most markets, you can find these pill vendors who carry large conical funnels with individually packaged pills rounding out the cone all the way up their one and a half to two-foot height! Some are Flomax, some Tylenol, others Adderall, hydrochlorothiazide, and can include heart medication, blood pressure pills, arthritis medication, and others.

At first this may seem OK until one realizes that none of them is labeled for intended use. And people will purchase one or two pills without knowing what they are to be used for, because they believe pills are medication and medication will help one's maladies.

Edvy had finished his treatment in Wilmington by October 1997, though, and was ready to go home, back to his work and family. And no doubt he was extremely pleased to avoid the winter in North Carolina. It was a miracle for him. He says, "God is one who we can always count on if God wills it so."

By this time, building the missionary residence and guesthouse facility at Lakil was underway.

Chapter 10

Building Lakil

The chosen site in Lakil for the residence and guesthouse was two-thirds of an acre, not a full acre as planned. But the size limitation was the least of the problems. The reason? When surveyors arrived to survey the land and prepare it for building, they discovered the property was in the middle of a huge swamp. Only small areas of dry land remained near the beach and the main road.

Along what is called the La Gonave channel* of Haiti there is, in most places, a reef lying just offshore. In tropical areas reefs exist in a complex, symbiotic relationship between organic and inorganic microorganisms that deposit calcium carbonate that gradually builds up to form the reef.†

---

*The interior of the "hand" of Haiti contains the Island of La Gonave, and the area south of this island all along the "thumb" is the area referred to.

†Genny Anderson, Marine Science, Bottom Dwellers, Ch. 4.1.1, Coral Reef Formation, 2003. See http://www.marinebio.net/marinescience/04benthon/crform. htm. Interestingly, a marine geological survey group from the University of Tennessee visited the site near Lakil in November 2009, taking soundings of the coral reef and ocean floor along our facility. We saw them but didn't know what their purpose was. After the earthquake, they came back to do more soundings and discovered that the sea floor had elevated 42 cm, about 16 ½ inches. The coral heads emerged and promptly died as the oxygen-rich air overwhelmed the living matter within.

As it formed along Episcopal Beach, the reef acted to prevent severe beach erosion, so that the beach behind the compound changes very little. However, inside this area along the section between the beach and the main road is a low area that often gets both fresh and ocean water flowing into it.

The narrow swampy areas north of the lagoon (where Episcopal Beach is located) lying along the shore for two or three miles are less prone to the same salinity. With the reef close inshore and the swamp inland about twenty to forty meters, there is a perfect breeding ground for all sorts of aquatic life—plants, microscopic animals, and huge areas where mosquitoes and other insects wait for unsuspecting humans.

At Lakil, and with the protective reef close by, there was not much erosion. But the question remained whether the site could suffice for the purposes intended since a lot of land fill was required. The basis for the decision to go ahead and fill the swamp has been lost to history. But, for nearly a four-month period during the latter part of 1997, more than one hundred truckloads of large rocks followed by smaller rocks were dumped into the swamp to provide sufficient fill to allow for a substantial pad on which to build the compound.

The compound was to consist of three buildings—residence, guesthouse, and kitchen/utility, plus a small outbuilding. The design called for the two larger units to be 20 feet x 40 feet and the smaller one 20 x 20, and for all buildings to have two stories. This meant there could be living quarters for guests and missionaries upstairs in the two larger buildings, along with a large kitchen next to the guesthouse, and adequate storage, a garage, and apartments downstairs, one under the guesthouse and the other under the kitchen.

Haiti Fund board members pitched in with donations, expertise, and design guidance; a can-do spirit permeated everything. This was because they were concerned for the difficulties Rodney and Sharyn had had in their tenure working with CODEP with government instability, shortages, and other complications, especially adequate, safe housing.

The designers wanted to make this facility as good as anything then available in Haiti, plus it was to be entirely self-sufficient in power, water, and waste treatment. A drilled well hit a good source of freshwater at 120 feet of depth, with no migration of seawater into the source or from the surface swamps on both sides after the rocks and gravel fill had stabilized the area. It had a submersible pump that could be pulled and replaced fairly simply.

A gray-water system throughout the facility was unique in design (certainly in Haiti) for the times. The freshwater system had several redundancies, from well-water treatment with chlorine to water softening to take out hardness to UV sterilization. Next was a reverse-osmosis treatment system for drinking water that was state-of-the-art for the time. Finally, the drinking water would hit another UV sterilizer before being sent to faucets around the facility.

Sewage was to be pumped into a large self-contained septic tank so that it could withstand any disturbances and would likely never fill up. (This proved to be the case; after sixteen years the septic tank had never been pumped out.)

Electrical systems were also redundant and could provide power under a variety of conditions. There were two diesel engines, one an installed spare so that they could have power from either; if one needed repair, the other could suffice until the first unit was back online. They could be operated alternately so that the number of hours on each engine could be kept low.

Both fed a transformer that changed the current from 240 volts AC to 120 volts AC. Power could be used directly from the generator as a 240-volt source. Since the well had a 240-volt submersible pump, there was a thousand-gallon tank that was filled whenever the generator was running so there would always be fresh water.

An inverter was installed under the garage under the residence quarters so power could be used from storage batteries when the generators were not running, enabling people to use power anytime. These batteries stored enough power to provide current for normal use that did not require the diesel generators to be run more than six to eight hours per day.

One of the sponsoring churches donated solar panels that provided a supplementary source of power to charge the batteries, so after the facility was up and running normal power consumption did not require either diesel engine to be run more than two hours in the morning and an equal amount at night. A secondary use for the solar panels was for power to run aerators in the fish hatchery.

The hatchery was built in conjunction with the Marine Biological Laboratory in Woods Hole, MA. They supplied considerable expertise in advising CODEP on how to provide tilapia species as a prime source of protein for CODEP participants. Since the solar panels and batteries provided electricity twenty-four hours a day, they would provide sufficient oxygenation so that fish brood stock could live through extreme weather events in case there was an interruption of power.

This was not an unreasonable logic train—after all, the country and the project had lived through several years of fuel shortages and delivery problems. So there was every reason to believe that, although the diesel engines were working fine, there might well be a dearth of fuel to run them.

In the fall and early winter of 1997 the landfill project was complete. In January, a young John Thienpont arrived with his Haiti Fund Board member father, Russell, to lay out the foundations of the three buildings. They stayed at the Hôpital Ste. Croix guesthouse. With Rodney to translate as needed, John and Russell began to lay out the foundation of the new facility.

Russell left after a week or so, and John stayed at Christianville where Rodney and Sharyn lived. Rodney would take him to Lakil on his way to the project. It was a long slog—for the next two months John labored to get forms made and put into place, rebar tied, and concrete poured, plumbed vertical and tight to avoid any leaks. Often, up to twenty Haitian workers were available to John, with ten of them regular nearly every day. When doing a large pour, there might be up to ninety or one hundred people to carry water, sand, gravel, and concrete, and in almost all cases they were coming down from the project to assist.

A diesel generator was installed to provide the power to run the tools, concrete vibrators, and a variety of other things, including the well, which they drilled just prior to John and Russell's arrival. John quickly learned the basic Kreyòl words for essential things—*matto* (hammer), *clou* (nail), *vis* (screw), *tourno-vis* (screwdriver), *tourno-vis letwal* (Phillips head screwdriver), etc. So he was able to get along quite well. He had a cook who came in and fixed breakfast and dinner, so he was able to snack during the day and had no problem.

"It worked great," John said, "because after just a few weeks I was able to move into a sort of apartment on the first floor of the residence. Of course, there was no electricity at night, but I had mosquito netting and slept well. It was while I lived at the compound and Rodney and Sharyn were gone that I pretty much learned Creole."[*]

---

[*]*Personal telephone interview with John Thienpont, August 23, 2015.*

As the year went on, progress began to show. Every other week a crew would come down to work on various systems—electrical, water, carpentry, and always the pouring of support columns, floors, more support columns, and even transverse columns that stabilized the building.[†]

[†]*Following the January 2010 earthquake, a significant aftershock occurred one evening during the visit of a damage assessment team, and the transverse columns did, in fact, stabilize the entire building.*

John welcomed the various people who came down to bring their specialized skills: Don Mills and Jim Sylivant[‡] on the electrical systems; Bas Snider from Midlothian, VA, who owned a plumbing supply business and installed the intricate and excellent water treatment systems; Bob Cacciotti, also from Midlothian, who fabricated the clamps for the solar panels; and many others. Welders, masons, plumbers, carpenters, and even those enthusiastic but without craft skills came, if for no other reason than to be gofers. The spirit and élan of the visiting people were incredible.

[‡]*The cooperative nature of the people who worked on the Lakil design was welcomed warmly. People from different, and often competing, companies worked together harmoniously. As a result, the quality and expertise that went into the design of the systems put in place at Lakil was excellent.*

One of John's finest memories is the groups who came from Charlottesville, VA, to do the carpentry work: "Jack Stoner did the roofs; they came and knocked out the guesthouse carpentry during one trip, and they stayed in tents right on site. When they came back to do the roof and finish the guesthouse, they didn't quite get finished, so we finished that up after they had left. Those guys were pretty amazing."

No experience of living in Haiti would be complete without a hurricane. Sure enough, in September of 1998, Hurricane Georges formed off the Cape Verde Islands in the Eastern Atlantic Ocean. It became a Category 4 hurricane that caused severe destruction as it traversed the Caribbean and the Gulf of Mexico in September 1998, making seven landfalls along its path.

Overall, Georges killed 604 people, mainly on the island of Hispaniola. By the time it arrived in Léogâne, Georges had weakened, but it still brought heavy rainfall across the entire country. John put it this way: "I went and stayed at the hospital in Léogâne, we hung out, and it rained and got a little breezy, but when we woke up it had flooded a lot of Léogâne, people's houses were washed away, and one bridge had been washed out. Lakil was fine; there was a big mudslide in one area, but Lakil fared well. It is a sturdy building; that's for sure."

The issue during hurricanes in Haiti is always mudslides caused by the lack of vegetation in the mountains. The immediate effect of hurricanes is the loss of life and homes, animals, gardens, and destruction of what little infrastructure exists in Haiti. However, the longer-term effect is much greater, since a few months later, people begin to starve because the destroyed crops (bananas, plantains, beans) are not available to eat.

Hurricane Georges notwithstanding, the construction of the facilities at Lakil continued to progress. Rodney and Sharyn needed to leave their place because Christianville needed the apartment the Babes occupied. By the middle of October, the Babes were able to occupy the residence quarters at Lakil while the guesthouse building continued. By mid-November, the guesthouse was completed. There was even an outside shower stall behind the guesthouse that could be used by visiting Episcopal priests who wanted to continue using the beach.

By Thanksgiving, John was nearly finished with his final checklist, and when he left in December, he could be proud of a job spectacularly done and deeply appreciated by Haiti Fund, the many people who had helped with the construction, and especially Rodney and Sharyn. The facility now housed the missionaries, and the guesthouse was ready to open for business.

A view of the completed facility at Lakil from the main road, looking across the swamp which borders the property on both sides. Missionary residence, guest house, and food preparation/intern residence can be seen.

Haiti Fund, Inc. now had a facility on Episcopal Beach property owned by the Episcopal Diocese. The contract already was signed by Jack Hanna and the bishop. Haiti Fund, Inc. had the rights to: "the use, control, and operation of the compound exclusive of the bathhouse and shower facilities shall be by Haiti Fund, Inc. for so long as it deems it necessary for the successful operation of CODEP or other projects designed for the benefit and betterment of the Haitian people."[†]

---

†Agreement between the L'Eglise Episcopale d'Haiti and Haiti Fund, Inc. signed by Bishop Duracin and Jack Hanna in 1997. This contract was in English, not French (the official legal language of Haiti), and was not notarized or dated. Such was the naiveté of Haiti Fund in the early days. This contract would one day become the focus of a dispute that would change the entire perspective of CODEP and Haiti Fund.

Haiti Fund, Inc., now had an official residence and a long-term commitment from the Episcopal Diocese to use it. It was more like a long-term license to continue working in Haiti. The expectation was that at least another ten years would be required to finish CODEP.

Who knew what additional projects could be done "for the betterment and benefit of the Haitian people" after that? The skies were blue and sunny; storm clouds had not started to gather, but in time they would.

Chapter 11

Expanding to Gwo Mon

Jn Sémé Alexandre walked several times a week from Kafou on the outskirts of Port-au-Prince to Duklo. He walked through a vast area southeast of Leyogàn that had a relatively sparse population and was essentially a barren desert. When you go by pickup truck to Léogâne and then to Darbonne (a small community about four miles southeast of Leyogàn), you notice how different things are.

Darbonne was the birthplace of Madame Duvalier, Baby Doc's spouse, and is the center today of some rather fierce political demonstrations during elections and periods of instability. This is where the health workers had done the survey for Jack Hanna years earlier.

A large sugar mill built by the Cubans stands in Darbonne. It is rarely operational because the capacity of the refinery far exceeds the capacity of the local sugar cane farms to supply it with raw material. As a result, except for a couple of months a year, it stays shuttered and rusty, a blight on the landscape offering far fewer jobs than they no doubt expected.

As you come into the center of Darbonne, the road turns at a 45° angle to the right and heads to the Rouyonne River, which is about two miles south and is the main river running through Leyogàn. Turn left 45° and the road takes you to the Momence River, a much larger river, but it flows northerly between Léogâne and Gressier to the north coast above Léogâne.

When you reach the Rouyonne (only in the dry season, because the river is unnavigable at other times), the banks are noticeably some fifteen feet above the riverbed in places. It flows at this point in a westerly direction toward Léogâne and under a newly constructed bridge (built in 2009, just before the earthquake) and flows to the south end of the city of some 200,000 people.

The Rouyonne is smaller than the Momence by far, but at that time it had a tendency to overflow much more easily. It is flat, wide, and almost completely silted in. At most points, it is at least one hundred meters across and narrows as it reaches Leyogàn.

When the rains come in April and last for six or more months, the river is constantly full of brown, silty, rapidly flowing muck. It is the main source of water for many families living within a couple of miles, and one can imagine that once water is collected and back at home, it must sit for an hour or more to allow the silt to settle so it can be used.

During the dry season, at the entry point south of Darbonne, pickups can enter the riverbed, turn left, and follow the wheel marks of other vehicles. The pathways wind their way back and forth along the riverbed, crossing small rivulets and meanderings on the way upriver. There is typically water year round in this part of the river, so you must be careful not to get too far off track, lest you get stuck, or worse, fall into a water hole deep enough to envelop your vehicle.

It is hard for Americans to appreciate the difference in perspective on what a river means to Haitians. The breadth of uses of Rouyonne River water is much more than we imagine, for it is life giving to families living nearby.

Some people collect water in five-gallon pails to take to their homes—a task that mostly falls on the women and girls, and is done at least once per day, sometimes more.

You will see people washing their clothes—again typically a task delegated to women—in the muddy water. First Haitians pile up sand around a circular hole; the sand filters the water to make it a bit cleaner—one hole for washing, one for rinsing, and usually a large rock close by to use as a scrub board. Once the clothes are soaped up, scrubbed, washed, and rinsed, young girls carry them delicately to the riverbank where they will spread them out over small bushes to dry in the sun.

Filling water containers for drinking is another use. The sand-walled "filter-pools" collecting water from the riverbed is considered to be adequate filtration for drinking. To American sensibilities, however, it is hard to imagine that these methods work well. Already contaminated from above by a variety of pollutants, drinking water is assumed to be better because of the bed-sand used to filter it a bit before they put it into the pails.

Although I have traveled to Gwo Mon at least thirty times since I have worked in Haiti, I have yet to see a significant change in this practice. There are regular governmental warnings, publicity campaigns, and even a series of text messages to emphasize sanitation. Using *dlo tretè* (treated water) is stressed everywhere, but the culture is slow to accept it. Cholera, typhoid, and other maladies are common, and there is little understanding of the possible causes, with contaminated water being a major factor.

Farther along on your drive up the river, you will see people bathing, usually in groups of two or three, separated by gender. Often when the women finish the washing, they will wash themselves, conserving the soap they have used to wash the clothes. They then put their clothes back on, after wringing out the rinse water.

These clothes dry quickly in the sun, so by the time the family gets home with baskets of clean clothes on their heads, the family is clean, the clothes they are wearing are clean, and they are set for a few days. My sense is that the typical rural family in this area has two or maybe three sets of clothes per person, so they do the washing every three or four days.

Farther up (or down) the river you see people taking care of bodily functions—defecating, urinating—using the river for washing away bodily wastes. Latrines are common near the houses, but people who live close by use the river instead. It is usually easier, there is no continuing smell, and they don't have to build a new latrine every few months. They view it as more sanitary. We would differ.

All this is a matter of perspective. Latrines are simple holes in the earth set some ten or twenty meters away from the house, with stakes around them and covered with leaves or banana-plant trunk halves to provide privacy.

When people have such needs and are away from the river or their latrines, they use space a few meters off the trail or road. In my experience, Haitian people have great respect for each other, knowing that others simply may not have any other options. So when you see nude or nearly nude bathers in the rivers and streams, no one is noticing. This is the Haitian way.

Although the culture is changing rapidly, only a few years ago women rarely wore anything but skirts and dresses, making it much easier to attend to personal matters when on the trail. Shorts and pants expose a lot more backside, as visiting American women were soon to learn!

As you continue up the river, it is not long before the mountains seem literally to come right down to the riverbank. They ascend slowly at first, and there are few houses, little vegetation, an occasional wild goat, no birds, a few insects, and once in a while people descending with their animals to the river for a drink. The entire area is called *Gwo Mon* (Large Mountain).

The ridge that is the north face of Gwo Mon runs for several miles in a roughly east-west direction, and both the Rouyonne and Momence Rivers course down through the crevices along the way. At the bottom, the Rouyenne runs westerly to the ocean and through Léogâne while the Momence turns northerly and runs to the ocean a few miles east.

It was on one of his treks through the area where the two rivers are closest that Jn Sémé began to think about expansion from CODEP's then location to Gwo Mon. It seemed there were a lot of areas that were barren of vegetation, animals, and importantly, people.

Note that Haiti is commonly said to have "ears," meaning that wherever you are, there are people just over the bushes or ledge who will hear whatever you are saying. Gwo Mon, though, was different— vast stretches of rising hills carved by small rivulets into a series of ridges that could and should have trees.

Land tenure, of course, had a huge impact. It was at this time that Jn Sémé and others conceived the notion of trying a new approach to getting access to land—by renting it. After discussions with Rodney and others, and noting that it had been done successfully in one or two places already in CODEP, Edvy and Jn Sémé went to the clerk's office in the city hall in Léogâne to find out who the land owners were.* This is a sometimes tedious affair, as often the land records conflict, are missing, or are in error.

Wise blans will let Haitians do these kinds of tasks. When a foreigner is involved, there is great risk that the process will be significantly complicated, as the bureaucrats will assume the blan has lots of money to be exploited.

These discussions spawned a whole new sense of possibility—could the project expand in spite of the issues surrounding land tenure? The project had grown rapidly, so there would come a time when the existing groups would run out of land. Purchasing land, as has been noted, required having all the owners sign off on the sale, and many owners no longer lived in the area of CODEP, or even in Haiti.

But renting might be considerably easier. As discussed at the end of chapter 6, people occupying the land (to plant crops) had rights conveyed to them through the legal system. The longer they had lived on or used the land, the more rights were conferred. The occupier of the land had the right to rent out the property for a few years, and renting was much cheaper than purchasing land.

If you could rent a piece of property for, say, ten years, there would be plenty of time for the CODEP process of reforestation to take place. CODEP could grow seedlings, plant forest trees, and later come back in and plant coffee, vegetables, and fruit trees like mango, avocado, lime, orange, cherry, and other varieties of fruits native to Haiti. Plus, rents could be paid up front, allowing the resident to have a pool of cash, and this would act as an incentive for the occupier to agree to a sufficiently long term.

There is a ridge-top footpath that leads out from the Jacmel Road at the top of the mountain directly down to a junction of several paths leading from the upper reaches of the Cormier Valley to Fondwa, a watershed that drains southward to Jacmel. One path leads off toward Fondwa on the right, another to the Cormier Valley on the left (including a fork off to Bwa Goch), and the main path continues dead ahead to Gwo Mon, a long transverse ridge extending several miles in both directions. The section around this crossroads is called La Ferrier.

This was a prime location, in that almost everyone traversed one or the other of the four paths to and from sources of water and local markets. There is constant traffic—pedestrian and horse, donkey, mule, and motorcycle; only pickups and large trucks are absent. Above it all is the Gwo Mon ridge, towering like a great giant, lazy and supine, stretched out like a rumpled sleeping bag toward Kafou and Port-au-Prince beyond.

In September 1998 Rodney and Jn Sémé noted that the La Ferrier area was completely barren of trees and looked like a desert. Small gullies intersected some areas. These often have trees, grasses, bushes, and a variety of plant life indigenous to the area. Not so with this plot, consisting of about twenty-two acres.* The plot was extremely steep, so crops regularly got washed out, and farmers were frustrated with their attempts to farm it.

As noted in chapter 6, the size of the land area is unclear.

There were three or four people living close by who had been planting beans on the property—so they had rights to use it in whatever manner they wished. Consequently, because they needed some ready cash, Rodney and Jn Sémé made a rental arrangement with them for the land for a ten-year period, with the full amount of the rent paid up front.

A typical pepinyè in the Gwo Mon sector. Note that each "plot" of seedlings is approximately one meter by five or six meters. Depending on the size of the plastic bag, the number of seedlings for each plot is large. This particular pepinyè has about twenty thousand seedlings.

Work began even before the rental documents were notarized and signed. As is the case for all worked land in Haiti, a variety of kinds of work began—driven by the need to fill hungry, empty bellies. Workers planted beans after using picks and shovels to break the hard dirt apart. Rodney focused on quickly planting trees. He posted guards so there would be no poaching as the seedlings grew. Proven methods of land preparation were used: large, rectangular holes with vetiver grass below and seedlings planted above. Later, coffee and a few fruit trees were planted to show what a mixed-species, reforested area could become.

As the FURREC and ADRA programs were still active, Rodney was able to deploy many people to the task. Hedgerows were dug along the contour so rains wouldn't wash out the Congo beans (also called pigeon peas), velvet beans, and holding grasses (including vetiver). Workers dug ditches at the end of 1998 and all during the dry season of 1999.

Because free-range goats were ubiquitous, the initial stand consisted of eucalyptus trees. But, because it was important to show how successful environmental reclamation can be, workers used liberal amounts of fertilizer, both when planting the seedling trees and afterward as side-dressing. Twenty-thousand seedlings for the project came from CODEP nurseries (pepinyès).

In one year, the trees had grown to double the size at the end of the prior year. Work continued into 2000, and soon after the rainy season started, the twenty-two-acre plot could be seen from the Jacmel road, a mile and a half distant. The plot was green and lush while all around it was a complete desert landscape.*

---

* In 2011, Jn Claude Bartholemy, one of the long-term CODEP people and one who has been an animator for many years, managed to rent property on the east (right) side of La Ferrier. Today a visitor can see the new trees that are about ten feet tall, and in a few years will be comparable to La Ferrier itself.

Work continued with transplanting coffee seedlings in the now-shady areas of the forest. These received a dollop of fertilizer too, and even insecticide, as new coffee plants are particularly susceptible to devastation by insects. The method of planting consisted of preparing a gallon-sized hole filled with compost, and after the coffee seedling was carefully planted, it was fertilized and an application of Sevin or a similar insecticide was applied. Also, guards were hired and posted at either end of the trail to discourage poaching.

One surprising development has also occurred—now some eighteen years after the first rental contract. The land has "sold"[†] twice during this period, and yet the trees remain. No one has chosen to clear cut them, and a few have been harvested for wood. The fruit trees and coffee plants are laden with produce, and people still walk through it daily on their way to and from Gwo Mon. When one goes into the forest, it is quieter, cooler, and much like a tropical forest with ferns growing profusely. You can even "call the birds in"[‡] to show visitors how much like a tropical paradise it has become.

---

† *Whenever "sold" or "rented" is used in quotes throughout this book, it means that access to the land has been secured but that the conveyance of title or secure rental access is not at all clear. Again, land tenure is a dicey proposition in Haiti, and when a group or individual obtains the property to use for reforestation, it is understood that there could be significant issues in the future regarding the legal niceties. It is my belief that these tracts of land are not disputed because we now know that the result is a significant improvement in the value of the land, which both renters and owners appreciate. Thus, it is possible to back into an understanding of how land disputes cannot be good for the long term.*

‡ *I first learned about calling in the birds from an HFI board member, Elizabeth Lusk, who has a master's in forestry from Duke University and who has worked as a naturalist for many years in North Carolina. Apparently, one particular sound is a universal alarm call for birds. It can be made by forming the lips as if one were to say the letter P but keeping the teeth nearly closed behind your lips. Then, whisper the sound psh, psh, psh several times and pause for thirty seconds or so.*

When birds hear this, they recognize it as a distress call and come to investigate. (Of course, one might recall why we use the term bird-brained when thinking about birds heading toward a distress call, rather than flying the other way.) In a few minutes, sure enough, birds of all varieties come around to see what the distress call is all about. The hardest part is keeping the visitors quiet for five or more minutes till the birds get there. Human voices spook them, so the experiment won't work if you have a talkative bunch!

Our fears that the land would be harvested by the owners as soon as the ten-year lease expired were unwarranted. Because of the overall success of CODEP, the people realize that reforestation makes a significant difference in the quality of life and the capability of the land and its people becoming self-sustaining, so the forest stays. That is not to say that some harvesting hasn't occurred—obviously coffee and fruits are harvested whenever they are ready, but residents have cut many trees for a variety of reasons without affecting the overall beauty and utility of La Ferrier.

Thus, as La Ferrier was becoming a reality, Jn Sémé began to look for land parcels in the sections north of the ridge. Plus, there were three animators who had an interest in working there, as there appeared to be many opportunities. Consequently, after 2000, Gwo Mon became part of CODEP.

Thus, CODEP moved into two new watersheds and provided for significant expansion of the project. Some of the longer-term animators, René, Bastien, and Enese, worked to seek out possible new lakou groups and parcels of land to rent in addition to the new lakous. One young worker who showed promise, Carlo Cenat, also began to work in the area. He would soon become an animator.

La Ferrier Demonstration Forest viewed from a distance of about 500 meters. You can see the barren land below and to the left of the plot. This photo was taken in March 2006, when the trees were seven to eight years old.

Chapter 12

Clement's Promotion

During the entire time that these events were taking place, the number of groups grew. Now there were more than twenty in Cormier, Fonde Boudin, Petite Harpon (known locally as Ti Apon, and thus written this way henceforth), and soon to be Gwo Mon. Younger people were encouraged to take leadership roles, and Clement, as the most promising one, got his share.

Clement's journey from finishing school in Port-au-Prince in 1985 to the day he started in CODEP was quite an odyssey. There was no work in DeLouch where he grew up. His father worked helping pour concrete in Santo Domingo, DR, and returned home only a few days a year. Therefore, Clement's future was dependent only on his personal diligence.

He sought jobs in Port-au-Prince, never an easy task. His sister, a seamstress in one of the Duvalier garment factories, lived in Cité Soleil. She had not had the chance to go to school like Clement. The place where she lived was nothing more than a shack, and she got very low wages, taking most of her check to pay rent and buy food for herself and her two young children.

He did not want that, so with few other choices, he asked a friend for work at the docks unloading containers. He got an interview with Autoritè Portuaire Nationale (APN), the national port authority. They needed good laborers, and Clement was hired, soon to have his indefatigable energy lead to a promotion.

He handled setting up areas where wheat, rice, sugar, sorghum, and other products could be stored safely until Haiti's creaky delivery system could move the goods around the country. It was a hard life: humid, long hours in the sweltering sun, large ships coming in and out of Port-au-Prince. There was always a push to unload them since demurrage on a container ship is exorbitant. The unloaded material still had to clear customs, but storing goods shortened the ships' delays and reduced their costs.

With the promotion, Clement learned to drive a forklift and a pickup. He got his chauffeur's license (not a simple process; it took nineteen months) so he could drive the vehicles on the dock. He didn't want to become a chauffeur, an even more stressful job with no definite future. (This was well before the death of Madame Jacques's son.)

During the entire time he worked for APN, there was significant political unrest, as Baby Doc Duvalier was deposed in 1986, and demonstrations, insurrections, and riots occurred weekly. The life was not easy, but Clement managed to begin living as young men often do, on the high side of life in Port-au-Prince going to dances and social events.

Soon he was cornered by a woman who apparently set her sights on this handsome young dock worker. She was eight years his senior, already had two children, and wanted him to marry her so they could begin a new life together. He was swept up in her enthusiasm, and soon they became a couple. I asked him why he would marry a woman eight years his senior. His response was simple and direct, "Because in Haiti, women with pretty faces like men who are younger."

The union eventually would produce a boy, Maradona (named after Clement's boyhood hero, the Argentinian futbol player) to add to the two boys she already had by other fathers.

After three years of working at the dock, Clement was stressed out from all the turmoil of living in Port-au-Prince: long hours at reasonable pay, but stressful. Plus, neither wanted to raise a family in Port-au-Prince, particularly in Citè Soleil, a hotbed of poverty and social unrest, to say nothing of the unstable political situation during that period.

So he went home to DeLouch and spent a year trying to find work. He got a job working on an occasional basis with the Pan American Development Foundation (PADF), a project initiated by John Kennedy to foster development through the Caribbean Basin Initiative, where agroforestry was a major thrust in Haiti during the eighties.

Clement could not find a regular job in DeLouch. He would travel to Port-au-Prince from time to time for piecework, but nothing was steady. During 1989, he found work with PADF helping farmers plant gardens of beans, manioc, and cassava. This lasted only for a couple of months, but since they were planting on the hillsides, he was able to use his port expertise and learn how to lay a level line with an A-frame, much like at the port.

He had good responses at the initial meeting with Rodney because of this experience. He had capably answered many of the questions, so Rodney asked him after the meeting if he would like to work for CODEP. He instantly said yes.

It was only a year later in 1992 that Rodney promoted Clement. He now led a group as a *chèf ekip* (team leader). Rodney culled about a dozen people who were already working and put them under Clement.

But Jn Sémé was unhappy with Clement's promotion. He had an angry conversation with Clement and complained to Rodney. Clement told Jn Sémé that his promotion could help make Sémé's workload lighter. Sémé was mollified (at least temporarily), so Clement continued working. He was also developing skills as a diplomat—an important leadership skill.

Rodney apparently liked Clement's energy and good work, because three months later he asked Clement to check on the other groups to see how they were doing. He especially wanted to know if they were following the established practices they were supposed to use: watering the seedlings, digging the canals and planting them with vetiver, and planting trees in the prescribed manner.

This angered Jn Sémé once again. He had loyalty to the people he brought into the project and felt this undercut his authority. Jn Sémé again complained to Rodney, but Rodney didn't tell Clement. He just said to go ahead and check up on all the groups.

This action was no doubt reasonable to Rodney for several reasons. Remember, simply traveling to the site was a huge undertaking, with traffic, the embargo, nonfunctioning governmental entities, and a scarcity of fuel. It would be a great advantage to have a trusted individual who would be able to give updates on an unfiltered basis regarding project tasks, objectives, and achievements.

However, Rodney's decision may also have sowed seeds of discontent that would be discovered much later in the project. Jn Sémé had been the project's first hire. He had attended two years of meetings with Père Racine, and he no doubt felt a sense of entitlement.

Jn Sémé may not have been aware of the organizational reporting relationships. He may not have even known that Rodney worked for the PCUSA and the Episcopal Diocese. But, he may have had the impression that Rodney worked for Jack Hanna, so he thought of himself as Rodney's peer, not subordinate.

It is easy for Canadians and Americans to miss this nuance, as we are used to having complicated reporting relationships. We regularly work with organizational matrices that need to be managed. Staff and line functions share responsibility for results. Setting and then accomplishing goals in a grid organization are common. We participate in 360° performance reviews and welcome them.

The patriarchal Haitian society is much more clear. The leader is leader and can make all of the decisions if he wishes. Typically the leader is the oldest and most senior person, and garners great respect. Therefore, to have a young man like Clement (who was twenty-six in 1991) providing information to Rodney was unusual.

Rodney wasn't even the most senior employee (that was Jn Sémé), and he worked for a US church denomination. Also, he didn't live in the project (neither did Jn Sémé, despite the logic trap this caused). All this was unconscionable to Jn Sémé. Therefore, the conflict proved to be the beginning of a long-festering sore which would erupt in a fury in 2005.

After only three more months, though, during which time the numbers of groups doubled, Rodney asked Clement if he would become an animator and manage several of the groups. Always on tenterhooks, this decision further inflamed Jn Sémé.

Compounding the problem was that Clement noticed a large number of people working on some land Jn Sémé was farming near Twaya,* which he knew was not project work.

Twaya, pronounced as no American or Canadian would expect, is chow-wa, in the unique system of phonetic spellings of Haitian Kreyòl!

Clement reported it to me this way:

I had noticed that Jn Sémé had four of his groups working in his personal garden for a whole month. I told Rodney, and he chewed out Jn Sémé, and Jn Sémé wanted me fired for it. This area was in Twaya near Madame Elyseé's fish ponds.

The people were supposed to be planting trees, digging ramps, etc. Later Jn Sémé saw me talking to Rodney about another subject and thought I was talking about his people working in the garden. But he thought I was ratting on him. He wanted me fired. Rodney checked it out and was very angry and refused to fire me.

This made Jn Sémé angry, but not nearly so angry as it made Rodney. He was ready to fire all the groups, but I talked him out of it. It was all right for me after that, since Rodney was afraid for himself and me because the people were so angry with the situation. That was when he asked me to come down to Lakil and do the logistics and live here. This happened in 1997, and so I worked both places. Jn Sémé was now happy.

So, as the construction project at Lakil got started, CODEP and HFI had a smart, loyal Haitian to live on site to keep things secure and to assist the variety of people who would create a magnificent living space out of a swamp.

Clement would live at Lakil for the next seventeen years.

Chapter 13

Forming APKF

At the end of 1999, as indicated earlier, both ADRA and MEDA began to reduce their flow of money and services to CODEP and Haiti in general. FURREC did too. MEDA needed to retrench, and Jn Claude Cerin came to visit with Edvy and Rodney about how to dissolve the relationship.

When MEDA first started making microcredit loans in Haiti, the issue was how to make the loans across the country in a fair manner. They also wanted to maintain good control over their disbursement, record-keeping, and repayment. Edvy learned these skills as part of his training. So, when MEDA began to withdraw, he was in a good position to continue the microcredit program if he could find an appropriate vehicle.

The program originally got started in CODEP because Rodney Babe had convinced the Haiti Fund board that it was important that CODEP provide seed money so the program would be a success. MEDA did this at the beginning. Later, as MEDA began to withdraw, there was money left over from CODEP's original contribution.

The solution was to form a farmers' loan organization licensed by the government. As Edvy started the long, bureaucratic process of filing papers to form what became known as the Asosyasyon Paysan Kômye Fonde Boudin (APKF), he was able to count on support in the form of a reimbursement from MEDA that had been originally sponsored by CODEP.

It took two years, and the result was that, in 2004, APKF gained official status as a grassroots farmer cooperative, complete with a board of directors, a plan for recruiting members, and even a building erected on land that Edvy owned about a mile from his home on Jacmel road. It was a good spot for such an organization.

Jn Claude Bartholemy, the president of APKF cooperative. Although Edvy Durandice is the executive director, Jn Claude and the others on the board ratify decisions Edvy makes. Jn Claude is a long-term CODEP animator who provided housing for interns for several years.

From the early days, APKF began to operate much like US organizations such as the Farm Bureau or Tractor Supply. The building had a small retail outlet stocking consumer goods, and a storage area for corn meal, rice, cement, steel reinforcing bar, wire, picks, and shovels.

There was no electricity, so the store was dark, but Haitians are accustomed to this. A person could buy rice, pliers, machetes, rum, gloves, cooking oil, telephone cards, and an amazing assortment of things farmers and residents would need on a regular basis.

Throughout the area, street vendors sell goods in many places alongside the road. APKF was quite a departure from the norm since it was an enclosed store. It was located thirteen kilometers up the Jacmel road from Kafou Kolas, and there were few other enclosed retail establishments all the way down to Jacmel, some thirty-five to forty kilometers farther on.

Making loans was the prime business of APKF. Someone could apply and qualify for a loan that might be for $50 US, and would expect to repay it in nine months, with a 2% per month interest payable during the period. Total cost: $59. It amounted to a 24% annual interest charge, usurious by American standards, but comparable to MEDA's interest rates.

The rate of loan failures is small. Each debtor must have four other Haitians as cosigners. That way, if there is any chance of default, the other four people will exert pressure and the loan will be repaid. Edvy's experience from his days at MEDA enabled him to make wise decisions about the people who were good credit risks.

Initially, CODEP had fronted about $30,000 to get the loan program started with MEDA. When the time came to close it down, they made an agreement that half the money due CODEP would go to Fonkoze (fon-kozay). Fonkoze conveniently had a local branch in Tom Gatto, a small village at the top of the hill. Haitian gourdes could thus be disbursed locally, without the need to change money in Léogâne or Port-au-Prince, which would involve potential security issues. The remaining half of the money went to Edvy for his fledgling volunteer cooperative and to build the APKF building.

Some went for the Animator Loan Program (Animatè Pwogram Kredi), APK. This was a huge step forward in development, as there was now an organization, owned and operated by local Haitians, that could provide a boost to entrepreneurial development.

Why didn't the money granted to MEDA go back to the people? Under the system that MEDA used, it was difficult to determine how best to return the money fairly, because people got different loans at different times. Some had more than one loan. And all loans were in various stages of repayment. As noted at the end of chapter 7, Edvy recommended that the money be deposited either in Fonkoze or used to continue the loan programs after MEDA shut down.

Within two years, an engine for economic development once again existed in the Cormier and Fonde Boudin watersheds—APKF. It had a founding board of directors: Edvy Durandice, Gilner Merizier, TJ Sanno, Jn Claude Bartholemy, and Madame Enese Medeé. All except Gilner were already animators working in CODEP, so there were good relationships already established with a strong interest in environmental reclamation along with microcredit.

One of the fascinating things about this organization is that it is egalitarian. A young APKF woman, Nadia, obtained a certificate in bookkeeping in Port-au-Prince. CODEP paid her tuition, so she does the bookkeeping both for CODEP and for APKF.

In the downstairs store are two clerks and a man who does all the heavy labor—lifting bags of cement onto pickups or donkeys, same with rice and corn and sugar. He wrestles with rebar and nails and a variety of other things. His name is Lueno and he is a small, energetic, wiry man who has more stamina than you would imagine. He lives right across the road and seemingly is always at APKF.

A few years ago, profits were sufficient to allow APKF to build a second story on the building, so now there is a stairway, a receiving area, a teller window for Nadia, and Edvy's office, with a conference room behind it.

Soon, APKF built a companion building with a commode and a cistern above so it could flush. The cistern is twenty feet above the water source at the road. It takes thirty trips with a five-gallon pail to fill it!* The building has a door facing the road, which is usually left open. It is the only flushing commode in a public place close to the road all the way from Léogâne to Jacmel, quite an accomplishment for APKF!

---

*Lueno and Larose Marie Carmella, the maid, take turns filling the cistern, back-breaking work in the best of times. Recently, one of the Haiti Fund Board Members, Jim Sylivant, and another engineer designed a well-conceived treadle pump (pumping water with foot pedals). It will lift water directly from the cistern under APKF to the upper cistern and do so in about fifteen or twenty minutes—pumping ten gallons per minute up the roughly twenty-five-foot rise.

The design calls for all materials to be purchased in Haiti for less than $50 US. The CODEP animators have an idea to make them as a CODEP branded product and sell them in Port-au-Prince to people who use cisterns filled with small electric pumps, which are notorious for not working, largely because of regular power interruptions in the city.

In Nadia's office upstairs are always a minimum of twenty-five cell phones connected to two 12-volt batteries. One of the APKF services is to charge cell phones for ten gourdes each (about 20¢). You find all sorts of people bringing their phones to Nadia for charging. They come in midmorning and return after noon to retrieve them, fully charged.

There even is a large solar panel outside with tiny wires running inside to charge the 12-volt batteries. A small business, lots of demand, a fair price, and it is fascinating to see how the entrepreneurial spirit works in Haiti.

In day-to-day operation, APKF functions much like a bank. The store downstairs accepts cash or writes chits (in the case of CODEP), and creditors pay the bill monthly. The credit program provides cash, some of which is kept in two large safes in Edvy's office.

Security is tight with bars on all doors and windows, double locks with steel boxes covering the padlocked latches (so someone with a sledgehammer can't break the padlock), and even bars around the receiving area outside the teller's window.

APKF is in a populated area and right beside the road, so there is little chance that a robbery would occur. In this part of the Leyogàn Komin, everyone knows APKF and the value it brings to the area in terms both of economic development and supply of needed items, so community cooperation and support is strong. This is the most important security feature of all.

That is not to say that APKF doesn't experience the regular problems that any bank or business encounters. Hurricanes or tropical storms cause a domino effect. For example, a farmer gets a line of credit to purchase seeds to plant a crop or to start a small banana farm. (Bananas are like corn; they grow only once, have one stalk of bananas, and then a new plant is planted the next year.)

The cyclone season occurs before the crops are fully mature. This can mean the loss of an entire crop. Then the banana loans are in default, APKF sees a shortfall in cash flow, and the farmer has a hungry family. Next, the situation gets worse because market banana prices rise because of the shortages—a cycle that can take months and years to overcome.

The systems in rural Haiti are simple, but they are interconnected and dependent. Thus one problem cascades through all of them, affecting the livelihoods of many families. A hurricane can take years to overcome.

In the twenty-five years CODEP has been in the area, there have been significant improvements in health, economic growth, nutrition, and the general lifestyle of people in the area, inside and outside of CODEP. But, a major natural disaster wreaks havoc to all the systems, and recovery takes time.

That said, the people rebound quickly, accepting their fate stoically and with renewed energy to start over, an amazing description to me of the resilience, faith, and confidence of these lovely people. APKF is at least one organization in Haiti that does wonders for the people it serves.

Chapter 14

The Interns Solution

Even before the guesthouse at Lakil was designed and built, the job of managing CODEP became increasingly difficult. The various programs (reforestation, microcredit, birth control initiatives, and education, to name a few) all required a lot of attention.

Also, Rodney and Sharyn's jobs also included work for Hôpital Ste. Croix and responding to the bishop when he called. And the visiting groups kept coming, which required planning, scheduling transportation, and finding work for them to do.

None of these activities included the variety of other things that happen on a day-to-day basis at CODEP. "Because Haiti is Haiti" is a phrase that everyone who lives or works there knows, and it means any plan is subject to the vicissitudes of happenstance. Each and every day.

Pickup trucks break. Tires go flat—or worse, blow out. Other vehicles *gen empan* (get broken), and often they are large vehicles that block or nearly block the road. With two-lane roads, long lines form in both directions. People get out of their vehicles, leaving them vacant to walk forward to the spot to see what went wrong and to check when it will be fixed.

When the line is finally ready to move, not only are cars and trucks in front of you vacant, but both lines try to get through at the same time. Sometimes it can take nearly as long to get out of a breakdown once fixed as it did while you waited.

In the field, tools break and things are done incorrectly. Laborers get to the site on time, but when materials or tools arrive late because of a road blockage, they go home, and when you arrive, no one is there.

If this seems to you like a rather pessimistic viewpoint, you are right. In the five-plus years I have lived in Haiti, I've grown to understand that some days, things go right, and at the end of the day you swell with enthusiasm about how great things are. Then one of those "going-backward" days happens and pessimism is the watchword.

However, my style is to operate as if there is a fine line separating the two contingencies, and if you maintain an understanding that things easily can go either way, life in Haiti is not only tolerable but is richly enjoyable.

Another kind of daily time consumer is unplanned visitors. People stop in to say hello. They have heard about CODEP and someone told them where to go to find the project leader. (It is uncanny how people can find you in the mountains, even off in a fairly remote area of the project.)

Other missions know of CODEP, and they encourage visitors and Haitians to see what CODEP is all about. Other missionaries often take a few days away from the mission, and (particularly when the guest-house was new) they stop by to visit, stay over, and swim in the ocean.

While this may sound insensitive and short-sighted, it is a real issue when there are large demands every day for the missionaries' time. Also, as has been pointed out before, the organizational structure that Rodney and Sharyn operated in was, at best, complex. With at least three entities needing attention—PCUSA, the bishop, and Haiti Fund—there was rarely a time when either one of them could focus on a single issue unless it was an emergency.

As early as 1996, Jack Hanna and Rodney talked about a way to ease the burden of being CODEP project director. For example, there were problems in Bigonè, the initial project target village. When the Léogâne priest responsible began to work with the Bigonè people and the headmaster at the school, things began to improve.

This, in turn, led to a discussion between Jack Hanna and the PCUSA about how Rodney and Sharyn could get some assistance. One early trial was with a young man who was sent by the PCUSA to help out, but the chemistry was not good so he was assigned to teach at Bigonè. Soon he was recalled and sent to Nicaragua.

Later, after the compound at Lakil was built, another young person, Chet Morrison, a Peace Corps volunteer who was a specialist in agroforestry, stayed with the Peace Corps but worked in the CODEP project. He had to learn the language, of course, but as he progressed, he was able to work in the relatively far-out areas of Bwa Goch and Gwo Mon, which helped Jn Sémé and the others get that area of the project started.

Rodney had had a serious auto accident in late 1994, and although now healed and able to work full time, he was not able to get to areas of the project well off the road, certainly not to Gwo Mon and Bwa Goch. So, having Chet involved in helping start work in Gwo Mon and Bwa Goch was a real asset. The fact that he was an agroforester was an added benefit.

The idea of having interns assist in a variety of ways within the project was attractive to both Rodney and Sharyn and the full Haiti Fund board. Chet's term lasted through the end of 2001, so a campaign to find interns to help in CODEP began in earnest in 2002. The discussions led to some basic standards.

Interns needed to come for periods from three months up to a year, maybe longer. They should have a college degree in agriculture or cultural anthropology, and should want to work with reforestation. Alternatively, they could teach in the schools supported by CODEP or help host visiting church groups. Of course, learning the language was the first requirement.

More than eighteen months after Chet finished his term, two recent college grads came to Lakil to start their year of internship. Jamie Rhoads was one, a cultural anthropology graduate from Appalachian State University in Boone, NC, who was raised in Cary, NC, but had spent time on a farm in the Shenandoah Valley of Virginia. The other was Clark Scalera, a Davidson College (NC) graduate from Tampa, FL, who wanted to gain international mission experience and could teach English at the Siloe School, which was supported by CODEP and located in the heart of the CODEP.

They spent a couple of months learning Kreyòl from a local lay preacher who spoke no English, essentially a form of total immersion. Soon they moved up the mountain, Jamie to Bwa Goch and Clark to a home close to Siloe School. Pastor Dures, the headmaster at Siloe, was pleased to have a blan teacher.

Three months later, they were joined by Frank and Becca Harmon, who came to work in CODEP after Frank graduated with a master's of divinity degree from Pittsburgh Theological Seminary (Presbyterian) whose International Mission Initiative is well known as a source of Presbyterian missionaries around the world.

They moved into what was now being called the "intern apartment" at Lakil and began to acquire Kreyòl. A month later they moved up the hill to live in the upstairs apartment of an animator, Jn Claude Barthelemy. This apartment was unique in that it had a commode and a cistern on the roof so they could shower and not have to use an outside latrine. Frank worked at Siloe, and Becca found a variety of things to do, happy to be in the midst of the project itself.

All four interns were able to go back to Lakil on the weekends to do laundry and refill a five-gallon bottle of purified water. None of the housing facilities in the mountains had any electricity, so it was pretty stark for them except for these weekend breaks.

Although Frank and Becca came with the notion of helping to host groups at Lakil, few groups were coming to see CODEP because of the political situation. Jn-Bertrand Aristide's term was problematic, and there were riots, strikes, and demonstrations that were becoming more and more frequent each week. So everyone was certainly more safe living in a rural area up the mountain.

By February, things deteriorated even more. Rodney and Sharyn had left for a long-planned visit to the US, and all four interns were alone in Haiti during the last week of February when Jean-Bertrand Aristide's downfall was imminent. They needed to get out.

Immediately.

All managed to get scheduled on an American Airlines flight. However, they had to travel to Port-au-Prince to board the flight. Deciding the best time to travel to the airport wasn't easy, as there were daily riots and demonstrations with burning tires and often, shots fired. Fortunately, their trip was uneventful.

A major issue was that neither Frank nor Becca had their passports. When Rodney and Sharyn left, they had dropped them off at the US embassy in Port-au-Prince for renewal. They couldn't leave without the passports. A close friend of CODEP, Pastor Leon Dorleans, who runs an evangelism ministry in Citè Soleil, let all four interns stay with him at his house near the airport.

He took Frank and Becca personally to the US embassy (located in those days close to the national parliament buildings, and therefore, close to the demonstrations). He stayed with them all day until they retrieved their passports.

In the end, Frank, Becca, Clark Scalera, and Jamie Rhoads all made the flight, which turned out to be the last American Airlines flight to leave Haiti before the airport was closed until order could be restored.

The entire month of February had been a rapid conclusion to a festering wound that had wracked Haiti for a year or more. Several months prior, a local gang leader from Gonaïves was found brutally murdered. He had headed the Cannibal Army (perhaps one of the least inspiring names for a grassroots political movement!).

His brother took over, vowing to get revenge on Aristide, who he believed had arranged the murder. The gang was renamed the National Front for the Liberation of Haiti. In early February, they took over Gonaïves by force, and less than three weeks later captured Cap-Haitien, Haiti's second-largest city.* By the end of the month, the rebels were threatening to take Port-au-Prince, the seat of government.

---

*For more on this topic, the reader can find a thorough discussion of those times in Haiti in a book by Peter Hallward, (2007). Damming the Flood: Haiti, Aristide, and the Politics of Containment. London: Verso Books. p. 210. ISBN 1-84467-106-2.

Aristide decided to abdicate, and the US State Department flew him out of Haiti at his request for his own personal safety, initially to the Central African Republic, and later, South Africa. There is some controversy about whether it was an abdication or if he was forced to resign. There was a real threat from the rebels, and it is likely the US State Department pushed him to go if for no other reason than to avoid bloodshed.

However, there were people, including some members of the US Congress, who believed he was pushed out unfairly. Colin Powell, secretary of state at the time, talks of Aristide creating much of the problem himself. He was a second-term president* with an aggressive political agenda. This included a request for France to pay Haiti $21 billion (US) as reparations for the debt Haiti paid France following independence in 1804.

In Haiti the president is elected for a single, five-year term and cannot run for a second term. However, there is no rule against running for a second term, so long as it does not follow the immediate prior term.

Aristide's request, to say the least, was controversial and caused several governments to suspend relations with the Aristide regime. Like before, the chief justice of the Supreme Court (this time) Boniface Alexandre became provisional president, and things began to calm down. The UN passed a resolution following Aristide's abdication to provide a security force of one thousand military personnel, initially consisting of US, Canadian, French, and Chilean troops, but replaced within four months by a UN force called MINUSTAH. MINUSTAH is still in Haiti today.

Perhaps of equal importance in evaluating Aristides's government and coup d'état was that the election itself (in 2000) was disputed, and there were claims of deliberate voter fraud. Whether this can ever be proven is doubtful, but the Aristide government got off to a shaky start, in particular because of the issues and problems that were still in the memories of many Haitians from his earlier term as president.

I find that Haitians have a tendency to evaluate national leaders in terms of how they are affected personally. With the Duvaliers, there was fear of the Tonton Macoute. Aristide was removed in a coup at the beginning of his first term. An embargo on the replacement government followed. Consequently, there were shortages and more hunger. So, in Aristide's second term, the people thought that it would likely end up much the same way.

So it was June before any of the interns could think about returning to Haiti. By that time, Clark Scalera and Frank and Becca had elected to move on to other things, as they needed to find work. Clark's term was up in August anyway. Frank and Becca found jobs and moved from their home in Indiana.

But the idea of having interns to help with the project was a seed that had sprouted. Jamie was to stay at his house in Bwa Goch for another year, returning to the US to seek a master's degree in natural resources from Cornell University. He would return to Haiti later, live in Cap Haitien, and work for a company that makes peanut butter (a national and popular food) laced with medications that children would not otherwise get.*

Jamie has served for a few years as a board member of Haiti Fund, Inc. He has been a most welcome addition because of his knowledge and understanding of the Haitian culture, to say nothing of his fluent Kreyòl.

The company, called MFK (Meds & Food for Kids), originated in St. Louis when a pediatrician found it was a good way to get Haitian children sustenance and needed vitamins, etc. that they would not get otherwise. This is another example of an organization recognizing a cultural tendency and taking advantage of it, finding easy acceptance of the idea by parents, children, and government officials alike.

In the year that followed (2005) there were two other interns who arrived about the time that Jamie's second year was up. They came in March and May, respectively. Meredith Barkley was an early-retired journalist from Greensboro, NC. April Leese was a master's of divinity student from Pittsburgh Theological Seminary. She signed up for a three-month summer stint, and would later spend two years living in the mountains in the same apartment where Frank and Becca had stayed.

Just as things looked to be getting back to normal (May 2005), there was another political upheaval. The temporary government put in place fifteen months earlier was becoming less popular. More demonstrations and riots became the norm. The PCUSA decided to pull all the missionaries out of Haiti, which included not only Rodney, Sharyn, and Jamie, but also both new interns. April had only been in the country for about three weeks, so she hardly got started before everyone left in the middle of June.

One of the tragedies of the intern program was that the full measure of interns' contribution was never fully tested. Both Chet and Jamie were able to do reforestation and agriculture, and Clark and Frank taught in the school at Siloe.

But the value of helping to host groups was never proven, as few groups came because of the questionable political situation. So, Haiti Fund, Rodney and Sharyn, and even the PCUSA did not have a sufficiently valid test of the concept of using interns in CODEP.

Through all this the people of CODEP continued their work, APKF moved on with its mission of providing credit and supplies for farmers in the area, and the schools continued to function. In Haiti, folks are used to having such things as political instability as a regular occurrence.

As in the case of tropical storms and hurricanes, they adopt a stoic approach and get on with their lives. While this seems tragic and frightful for most North Americans, it is a way of life in Haiti, so one must proceed. Stoicism works.

APKF was now moving forward, and a variety of people worked there. I noted near the end of the chapter on the formation of APKF that there were a couple of fascinating people who worked in the storage depot. One was Larose Marie Carmella, or Nwèl. She seemed like a good candidate for the writer to interview as the CODEP "outsider" for this book.

I wanted someone outside of CODEP who had no visible source of income but who likely would have been helped by having CODEP's presence all around her. She seemed friendly enough and worked at APKF mopping the floors, hoisting five-gallon pails of water on her head to walk up to the topmost cistern on top of the bathroom building, and helping deliver all sorts of things to APKF clients who couldn't visit the store.

The next chapter begins the story of Nwèl.

Chapter 15

Nwèl (Noel)

A common Haitian phrase I mentioned before is that "Haiti has ears." This means that wherever you are, there is someone nearby who can hear you. Americans and Canadians forget this easily. We have air-conditioned cars and buildings, and our lives are insulated, literally, from the cacophony around us.

Not so in Haiti. Windows are open. Buildings are typically vented to let air blow through. People are usually outside except for sleeping. So, when I asked to talk to Nwèl, she naturally asked if we could visit on her porch. I presumed that it was an area where there wouldn't be so many "ears" around!

The reason to visit Nwèl was to talk about her life, her perspective, and what she felt about CODEP going on all around her, but in which she didn't participate. I wanted to know what she thought, whether her life had changed, and what her future was.

Nwèl walked briskly up the muddy path in front of me, her beat-up, two-sizes-too-large Croc knockoffs slipping in the muck. It had not rained since Sunday, but the ground is saturated everywhere here at the end of the rainy season.

She wore an old, black skirt with a zipper needing help from a large safety pin at the top, and a bright yellow blouse, too tight, and more than a bit worn. She chattered nervously as we walked up the hill on the narrow, mud-slicked path to her home.

I had seen her house once before when I was asked to visit a sick daughter who was having severe back pain. I remembered Nwèl's daughter, Patricia, was sitting in a chair crying silently, one leg perched up, the other curled at the ankle on the floor. Was I qualified to make any medical assessments? No. Was I capable of making a recommendation as to what to do about the pain? No.

So, why was I asked to see Patricia?

Because I am a blan, a foreigner, a leader of the project, and the assumption by most rural Haitians is that the blans know the solutions to all problems. So I talked to her, got nods through the sniffles, and she told me it was pain in her lower back.

Not being sure about what to suggest, I told her I'd let her know tomorrow. She nodded, wiped her tears away, and stopped crying completely. Apparently, just my being there and showing concern was helpful. Later, I made a phone call to an American nurse who works here and she told me that flank pain was common during menstrual periods. A couple of ibuprofen pills would do the trick. Now, as I walked along behind Noel, she thanked me again for helping Patricia.

Nwèl opened the door to the house—one room with a partition, so the back part had beds for the kids, and two single beds in front doubled as places to sit when company came. She took out two straight-backed Haitian chairs, rough-hewn with woven seats, and set them on the porch so we could look out at the view.

The view extended about ten feet to a concrete water tank and a bamboo-walled cooking hut placed close to the door where all rural Haitians cook, in pots, over open fires. This keeps the carbon monoxide moving when cooking—where the main staples are rice and beans, fried plantains, and the sweetest coffee you are likely ever to drink, dipped with bread.

Next to the cooking hut is a concrete cistern, which has PVC pipes draining from the tin roof. Washing hangs on two lines strung between the hut and the cistern. With four kids, and each one having only two or three sets of clothes, a wash hangs nearly every day. A tan, skinny dog lolls on the concrete floor of the porch, not interested in either of us, occasionally whacking at a flea or pest in his ear.

"We can sit here if this is OK with you?"* Nwèl said with a questioning look in her eyes. I sat, motioning her to do the same, indicating agreement. The nervousness persisted, so I took the time to explain the reason for my visit—to find out how people not in CODEP managed as CODEP grew all around them. (Only lakous which have access to land are allowed to participate, and certainly someone of Nwèl's stature and position would not have access to land.)

---

*Larose Marie Carmella, personal recorded interview transcription, first recorded on October 1, 2013. During the nearly two years when I researched this book, I interviewed Nwèl three times and followed up at least twice. Through it all, she remained modest, a bit nervous, but pleased to talk about her life and family; a perfect demonstration, from my perspective, of how most Haitians accept their fate in life as it comes, with a strong spiritual faith that guides them at all times.

I explained to Nwèl that it is important to tell the story of CODEP, but also to tell the personal stories of people who lived here before CODEP and who decided to stay, people whose lives have changed as a result. She was not working in CODEP, but her life has no doubt changed. For CODEP, its richness is very much in the stories of the people. And she was to be one of them.

The first step in this process was to ask for her full name and how she spelled it. She smiled, perhaps proud to be included, I thought. (Or worse, I realized suddenly, she can't even read or write and maybe I had made a gross error by asking her to spell her name.)

She said her name was Carmella Larose Marie. (Note that she said it like all Haitians do, last name first, then first and middle names. They sign their names the same way.) I didn't understand her pronunciation, and when I asked her again, she reached out for my notebook, took my pen, and wrote it out beautifully in longhand. That salved my guilt at being so bold as to ask her to spell her name, which was suddenly replaced with new guilt that I had assumed she was illiterate.

She went on explaining that Nwèl is her nickname because she was born on Christmas Day. Everyone called her Nwèl from the time she was an infant. Of course, Noel! This was another fascinating thing about this complex society with its nuances and mysteries that challenge those of us who are guests. And yet we have the privilege of living in this land to be welcomed and loved, in spite of our seeming strangeness to the natives.

I had known Nwèl for nearly eight years since I first visited CODEP in 2005. Nwèl had been there all along, working at newly-formed APKF as a combination custodian and a runner for things forgotten. Most of the time Nwèl went barefoot, as her youngest son (now twelve) invariably did. She has an amazing amount of energy no matter what the task.

The variety of tasks is hard for us to imagine—I've talked about carrying five-gallon buckets of water to the high cistern on top of the APKF toilet. But there are others, including fetching water for mopping the floors; separating trash to save all the organic parts that can serve as food for pigs, cows, and horses; making sisal ropes from feed sacks; wrapping new broom ends on sticks when the existing ones wear out or are too bent over to be usable.

When there are meetings at APKF and lunch is served (in rural Haiti it may be the only meal of the day), Nwèl is the one who hikes up the half-mile slope to the cook's house. She helps fix the meal and then, in two or three trips, runs down the hill on the footpath. This, while carrying hot, large pots of rice or beans on her head which will feed more than a dozen people, not counting all the employees of APKF, who also share in the largess.*

---

*Part of the mystique of the culture is that rank, social standing, and public perception are huge factors in people's lives. The rationale might be, since CODEP is a successful organization and has time to hold long meetings once a month, then it is proper for everyone to know that they have enough wherewithal to provide a good meal at the end of the meeting.

The nuance of this is that the folks who work at APKF also get to eat everything that is left over (and of course, enough is prepared so that there will be some for everyone). Nwèl works rain or shine with an ebullience that is astounding. This is why I wanted her to be one of those interviewed. Such work seems to both energize and animate Nwèl, and today was no exception.

As we sat on the porch looking at the water-tank/cooking-hut view, I showed her my handheld digital recorder, explaining that I could easily pick up her voice and she was free to respond in any way she wanted. She seemed eager to talk, so I began by asking how old she is. Forty-six. (In rural Haiti it is not an issue to ask a woman her age.)

We talked at length about her family, her life, and the variety of things that were of interest to her on this day. Born and raised close to Duklo, she is happy to be working. Her parents both died when she was a young girl, her mother when she was seventeen and her dad two years later.

Larose Marie Carmella—Nwèl— born on Christmas Day 1968. Nwèl tries out the new treadle pump. Women are particularly suited to use this device, as they soon learn to lean side to side and the pumping happens naturally with hardly any effort. Men, thinking it is like a StairMaster, push too hard; the valves weaken and soon the pump no longer works!

She accepts this as a way of life, explaining that many children's parents lost their lives during those days; her voice trailed off. I was alerted to perhaps explore this later. She was in her late teens at the end of Baby Doc Duvalier's rule, so perhaps she didn't want to say more. Lèyogàn was a political hotbed, then and now. Yes, I would ask later.

She talked about her hopes and dreams. They center on her children, not herself. Her oldest, a mechanic in Kafou, near Port-au-Prince, makes good money working on cars, but she wishes he lived closer. Her husband works in both Lèyogàn and Port-au-Prince and stays with her son when he has to be out overnight in Port-au-Prince.

She wants the family to be together all in one place but understands that this is the way for many families living in Haiti. Her two daughters are both in school at the new CODEP Duklo Middle School, both in the same grade, though they are two years apart. They make high marks, and she washes their school uniforms every other day since each girl has only one.

The school holds classes from seven thirty to twelve thirty each day, often including Saturday, from the first of October through the end of June.* Middle schools are not prevalent in the area, which is why CODEP decided to have one. The staff was chosen carefully by a partner and friend of CODEP who runs a successful one-to-thirteen unitary school in Lèyogàn.

---

*As this is written, in 2015, Haiti has changed the start date for all schools in the country to start on the second Monday of September. By starting a month earlier, without changing the end date in mid-June, the system can accommodate disruptions during the fall such as tropical storms and hurricanes. Not unlike snow days in the US.

The Haitian government provides few public schools. Thus almost all schools are private, particularly in rural areas. Standards for faculty are surprisingly weak, and many teachers are little more educated than their students. The Education Ministry traditionally provides required end-of-grade testing for fifth, ninth, and thirteenth-grade students.

They are graded pass-fail and, to advance to the next level, students must pass. If they fail, they are required to wait a year to take the test again.† The cost for the testing is not inexpensive, so it is an important mark for the sponsoring school to have a high percentage of students pass. Our partner's school has 100% passing rates, so Nwèl is optimistic for her two girls.

---

†Recently, the Ministry of Education changed the testing system to test only at the end of the ninth and thirteenth grades.

It is a requirement that schools operate for a minimum of two years before end-of-grade testing can occur, and a certain performance percentage of passing grades will set the standard for whether the school is seen as desirable. This means it is three years before the first testing can occur.

For Nwèl to put her girls in the school was a bit of a crap shoot. Tuition is three hundred Haitian dollars a year (1,500 HTG), less than $40.00 US, not counting the school uniforms. This cost is for the first year; after that it goes up significantly. This may not seem like much to Americans, but Nwèl's compensation is about $35.00 a month. Two months and ten days' salary for tuition for the girls—a steep price in any country.

Time was short, so we agreed to talk again. Nwèl said she was glad to talk about her family, her work, and all the differences CODEP had made in her life. We would talk more as time went on.

And I wanted to get back to her sadness about her parents' deaths. I sensed there was more if she would only open up.

· · · · · ·

The last few chapters have broadly discussed the period from 1997 through about 2004. As noted in the introduction, this book is not a specific chronological unfolding of CODEP. Rather, I have taken broad periods and peeled back the layers to make the important lessons evident. These help us investigate sustainable development—what makes it succeed and what makes it fail.

As you will see, by the end of 2004 there were several issues that became significant threats to CODEP and its successful work over fifteen years. There was a strong possibility that it would fail, or that Haiti Fund would fail and take CODEP down with it.

I believe two major factors caused this. First, the complicated organizational framework and reporting structure for the Babes inhibited communications and prevented common understanding among stakeholders. Doing everything in Haiti exacerbated these issues and made them more difficult to address and resolve.

The second factor was the loss of Jack Hanna and Rodney Babe without much planning for their replacements. In Jack's case, it was more of how the board was constituted during his tenure and how it needed to change upon his retirement. In Rodney's case, it was a lack of certainty about whether or when he would be reassigned by the PCUSA and not having trained a replacement. Both these men had significant knowledge and techniques in CODEP's successful system—institutional memory—which I will define in the next chapters. Losing that institutional memory was a huge issue.

First, let's deal with organizational issues.

Chapter 16

Organizational Challenges

We have seen that Rodney Babe's organizational reporting system was complex. As the project grew, this system had a more negative impact. Each domain that Rodney served had its own interests. So he had to communicate things to each organization independently, which was time consuming.

One of Jack Hanna's special skills was to keep people informed and up to date. He would regularly call on the bishop, talk with PCUSA representatives whose responsibility included Haiti, and keep Dr. Jack Lafontant, the Haitian director of Hôpital Ste. Croix, informed. And he kept Haiti Fund's Board of Directors in the loop on all things.

All this worked well so long as Jack was the president, CEO, and visionary. And since Jack had worked closely with the PCUSA and the bishop to conceptualize the project, his institutional memory of the history and developments of CODEP went unquestioned.

As if the Babes' organizational complexity weren't enough, their situation was exacerbated by the changing political scene in Haiti. Although the end of the nineties passed well, when Aristide won a second term in November 2000, there was a question mark about the future. It might mean that there would be political intrigue, perhaps violence, and even an expanded role for the thousand or so UN peacekeeping troops residing in Haiti permanently.

Still, everyone remained upbeat and optimistic about CODEP. So it was like a thunderbolt when the news came that Evelyn Hanna had developed cancer. Of course, it was a great shock for both Jack and Evelyn. It would test their faith in many ways, cause great reflection, and long hours of talking about lives well lived. With five adult sons, they would have lots of help.

So Jack would retire and care for Evelyn, no longer going to Haiti. But he was still available for advice and counsel. For HFI and CODEP, it was a minor organizational change. But it led to significant operational issues stemming from the complicated organizational framework:

- each entity continued to follow its own interests, but without Jack's coordination/information role;
- this increased the pressure on Haiti Fund to be sure its interests were protected; and
- conducting business in Haiti, never easy, became even more difficult as CODEP continued to grow in size and complexity.

Let's peel back each of these issues.

Each Entity Followed Its Own Interests

Jack's loss wasn't immediately felt by either Haiti Fund or CODEP, and things continued to progress. But without Jack's presence and hard coordination work, it wasn't long before slight cracks began to occur in the organizational foundation.

Nothing was deliberate or malicious; just a matter of the various entities following their own interests. Scheduling CODEP mission group visits is an example. The prime time for groups to come to Haiti is in the first quarter—it is dry, cool, and has fewer mosquitos! So many CODEP supporting churches choose this time to visit. But PCUSA sometimes scheduled events for their missionaries at this time, too.

For the Babes, any US trip provided an opportunity to see their daughters, who were in college in the US. It was reasonable for them to visit them when in the States. This meant, though, that the Babes could be gone from Lakil for almost a month.

Thus, it wasn't tenable to have the Babes gone from Haiti during prime time for groups. Interns couldn't host the guest groups without considerably more experience. And, there was nothing quite like having Rodney available to answer questions, provide nuances, and explain how the Haitian culture worked.

Separately, Bishop Duracin was beginning to make his presence felt in ways not necessarily conducive to operating the CODEP project. Dr. Lafontant, the first Haitian to head Hôpital Ste. Croix, was let go suddenly.

About the same time, a nursing school in Léogâne was starting classes, so there was a push by the hospital to direct groups' involvement in that direction rather than CODEP. Fewer visiting church groups with multifunctional interests were coming. CODEP now had larger groups than before, since few of the people had much interest in HSC and the nursing school.

Some development work was being done by the Haitian diocese. Although CODEP was about agricultural development and reforestation, the bishop had an interest in using it as a training tool. A new trade school was completed in Aux Cayes, west of CODEP.

I have been told the PCUSA was contributing up to a half-million dollars per year to the diocese for health, education, and agriculture. This included the Babes' salaries and support for St. Barnabas agricultural school located in the north of Haiti.

Also, the Episcopal Relief and Development group in New York was a major contributor to a variety of programs conducted by the Episcopal Church in Haiti—schools, hospitals, orphanages, and the National Episcopal University of Haiti (UNEpH).

So a lot of money was flowing into Haiti. This interested the bishop, who had a lot of ideas on how to spend it.

Ensuring Haiti Fund's Interests Were Protected

Organizationally, Haiti Fund was adjusting to no longer having Jack Hanna as the leader. Also, the other participants—PCUSA and EEH—were fully staffed and moving forward, not a good balance with Haiti Fund being understaffed. The HFI board always had had people from some of the early supporting churches. Different representatives would attend, and there was no particular continuity of people attending. Thus, different people developed different perspectives. This involved loss of what I referred to earlier as "institutional memory."*

As any organization grows, it quite literally "learns how to do things." Much of this is transferred to other organizational members by the people already in the know about how to do any particular task, for example. Most of it is not written down. Thus, unwritten rules develop.

Social customs, mores, procedures, and the local culture all get inured into the organization, and they create institutional memory. It can act (and does act most of the time) as both a controlling function and a productivity improver. So doing a particular job in a certain way gets to be the standard. Therefore, changing the standard must be a task of convincing the entire surrounding culture that the changes are needed.

———————————————

Thus, without consistent "memory" of the work of HFI or CODEP, board meetings became not a time for reporting, but times of seeking to understand what was going on, how to interpret it, and then deciding how to react. This was quite different from how the board had functioned from its inception. Instead of listening, taking notes, and perhaps ratifying a decision or two, attendees had to act like real board members. They had to make well-informed but often difficult decisions as a board. This required continuity, something the board lacked.

From Rodney and Sharyn's perspective, their attendance no longer complemented Jack's efforts. Now they were suddenly in the position of having to answer probing questions by board members who were trying to learn.

But it must have looked to the Babes like the board was suddenly much more prying. Board members also gave many more suggestions about how to do things in Haiti. Many of these weren't possible in the Haitian culture. Board members didn't understand this because institutional memory had been lost.

It wasn't that board members hadn't learned anything about CODEP. Most of them had visited. But now the role of a board member had changed. They had responsibilities to fulfill as board members in the harsh glare of making potentially huge mistakes. Not comforting or easy.

And, most important, HFI board decisions were often made without foreknowledge of what the Diocese of Haiti, or Hôpital Ste. Croix, or the PCUSA, or sometimes even Rodney and Sharyn would think.

Growing Complexity/Difficulty of Doing Business in Haiti

All these things were brewing in the large and growing pot that was CODEP in Haiti. Actions taken by any of the stakeholders might affect the others in large measure. However, decisions needed to be made. But the kind of collaborative understanding among the organizations that had been common under Jack's tenure now often did not exist.

Another example was the situation in 2004 when the interns needed to get out of Haiti fast. The PCUSA was not aware that HFI had interns in Haiti. Since the Babes were already in the US, no overseeing group was adequately concerned as the political situation deteriorated that February. No doubt the PCUSA's connections in Haiti could have made it easier for Clark, Jamie, Frank, and Becca to get out.

It was not that HFI and PCUSA were in dispute; it was just that there was no one charged with coordinating perspective and communication about such matters. In the end, it worked out, and afterward there was a special attempt to identify and provide coordination. But learning the lesson required a special crisis.

These three situations—each entity protecting its interests, ensuring HFI's interests were protected, and having to do them in Haiti—all caused significant problems for the Babes.

These problems are listed below. I've discussed each of them separately:

- Babes' reporting authorities remained unclear and poorly practiced.
- This led them to feel the need to become increasingly independent to accomplish their tasks.
- When issues or problems developed, each entity tended to try to get it resolved independent of the others.

Babes' Reporting Authorities Poorly Defined and Practiced

Evaluating performance, awarding merit increases, career counseling, and discussions of benefits and pension plans are part of a well-developed system within the PCUSA. All ministers and most mission coworkers are part of the program and requirements for annual appraisals, and specific times for gaining rest and relaxation are part of the program.

For whatever reason, my understanding is that these protocols were not adhered to consistently with the Babes, perhaps because of the demands on their time. Also, neither Haiti Fund nor the Episcopal Diocese regularly checked to be sure they were being done. This may have been due to Jack Hanna's retirement. But the reality was there was no consistency from the Babes' perspective.

Episcopal Church polity vests many personnel decisions to the bishop, who at that time willingly made them, but Rodney and Sharyn were not part of that protocol. And, because these practices were infrequent, it put the Babes in the position of needing to act more and more independently.

Need for More Independent Actions by the Babes

Rodney and Sharyn had grown to be experts in all matters involving CODEP. So they were the only ones who knew what to do in any given circumstance. Even though some board members had limited French, almost none had a facility speaking Kreyòl.* Therefore, Rodney or Sharyn had to be pressed into service as interpreters.

One of the board members, Jim Sylivant, spent a lot of time in Haiti. He had learned French while living in Provence in the 1970s. He was able to communicate in French and limited Kreyòl. In addition, as an electrical engineer, he was in great demand for a variety of missions needing guidance and assistance with design, maintenance, and operation of power systems, most of them independent of the power grid.

Jim also was needed to help design and implement the electrical systems at Lakil and was helpful to Rodney and Sharyn in this effort. He also worked closely with Hôpital Ste. Croix, where the systems were quite complex. However, he essentially was the sole board member with competent language skills.

This complex system of reporting caused Rodney and Sharyn to become demanding in getting their needs fulfilled to get project actions done promptly. They needed constant support (both with funds and with project supplies) to keep CODEP on the growth curve everyone wanted.

The Babes' growing independence was fine and needed. But some newer HFI board members didn't see this in the context of the overall situation the Babes faced. Again, a loss of institutional memory.

Resolving Issues without Consulting Other Entities/Stakeholders

When problems came up, the entity with the problem would resolve it. It was quick, appropriate, and necessary. There typically wasn't time to consult other affected parties. PCUSA would do its personnel reviews and tweak the pension plan. The bishop would occasionally come to the Episcopal parishes in CODEP for visits. HFI collected and sent money to CODEP for project tasks. Things worked. Problems got addressed. CODEP grew.

Groups from the States came to visit the CODEP project to see how their money was being used. PCUSA folks would come from time to time to check things out. Sometimes they would come to Lakil, stay over, and visit the project.

Other times Rodney and Sharyn were called to Port-au-Prince to visit PCUSA people, which invariably involved meetings with the bishop, too. Sometimes the bishop asked Rodney or Sharyn to attend a conference.

And the mission groups kept coming.

Rodney and Sharyn were pleased with how the project was going, but this created additional work for them. And the reporting system exacerbated the situation. This caused the pressure to keep mounting.

Chapter 17

Changing of the Guard

Chapter 16 dealt with the issues caused by the complex organizational framework that governed the work of CODEP. These issues were exacerbated by Jack's unexpected retirement. The board had to change both perspective and method of operating. These changes complicated the Babes' reporting structure even further. Getting things understood and accomplished became harder and harder for everyone.

This chapter deals with these same situations but reflects how the *people* dealt with them: how HFI tried to overcome many of these issues, how new people came in to help out, and the effect this had on the Babes, and especially, on CODEP. The broad issues were:

- how to manage Haiti Fund after Jack Hanna;
- how to aid Rodney and Sharyn as their assignments became more complex;
- how to do this in the face of changes in PCUSA and Episcopal Diocese of Haiti; and
- how to accomplish everything in the face of continuing political instability.

How to Manage Haiti Fund after Jack Hanna

Jack Hanna's decision to retire in 2000 to take care of Evelyn prevented him from going to Haiti, but he was still available for planning, board meetings, and acting in an advisory capacity as needed. Board member and lawyer Tom Heller agreed to make trips to Haiti in Jack's stead.

He agreed to carry on the work Jack had been doing. He visited Rodney and Sharyn, made courtesy calls on the bishop, and worked with PCUSA individuals who were in Haiti when he was there. The expectation was that things would be able to progress as before.

Wisely, during this period, the board consulted with Rodney and Sharyn and wrote a new set of strategic objectives to be sure the mission and vision were consistent with what the project had accomplished to date, and what was needed in the future.

The board of directors articulated Haiti Fund's mission and vision. The new mission statement clarified the role of Haiti Fund while the vision stated what it would look like when the mission was fulfilled. They were quite clear:

Mission: Cooperate with and assist the people of rural Haiti by initiating, funding, administering, and sustaining development programs aimed at increasing self-sufficiency.

Vision: A land of plenty in the mountains of Haiti where the people live in peace and have embraced a plan to restore God's creation. In this place, the residents enjoy good health, quality education, and economic stability so that they can live together as a thriving community of God's children.

At the beginning of 2001, the board decided it would be of great help to have someone specifically charged with managing HFI's interests, both in Haiti as well as in the US. A quick search found an excellent candidate.

Jim Pease was a member and elder of one of the key supporting churches of Haiti Fund, and most importantly, felt a keen sense of call to become executive director. He had a strong sense of mission, very close to that stated by Rodney and Sharyn. It was a nice fit—Jim was anxious to help.

He was welcomed by the board, and everyone had high hopes that Jim would be able to help in a variety of ways. He would focus on organizational issues. He would redefine roles of board members. Also, Jim would lead the effort to identify and recruit Volunteers-in-Mission (VIM).

The VIM effort was a new PCUSA program where (primarily) young people would be recruited to assist in foreign missions. It was similar to the intern program HFI wanted. It might solve the question of how best to use the guesthouse at Lakil, even if what to have groups do was still unclear.

Another issue was the need to provide for succession planning. Jack's retirement and the retirement of Charlie Fyfe, another long-term board member, created the need to think about board composition.

So, as Jim Pease started his assignment, there were rather significant issues to deal with. However, he had the confidence of the board, and his sense of call to the position was strong. He was motivated and spent most of his first year accomplishing a variety of objectives, positioning Haiti Fund to accomplish its mission effectively.

Aiding Rodney and Sharyn as Their Assignments Became More Complex

Jim visited Rodney and Sharyn, CODEP, and the bishop. He went to Louisville and worked out how the Volunteer-In-Mission program might work. The real issue was how best to host mission groups without taking significant amounts of Rodney and Sharyn's time. Need for help with the guesthouse was obvious.

What to do with the visiting mission groups was still not clear. As noted earlier, the concept of a mission trip had been particularly difficult as far as CODEP was concerned. Mixed groups came: Some were doctors visiting Ste. Croix; others came as mission visitors who wanted to see the variety of things the PCUSA was doing in Haiti.

CODEP was on the list too, of course, and after the guesthouse was completed more people came. But project visits were observational, and the long-term issue remained: *Groups wanted to come to work. But work projects fly in the face of development.*

Rodney and Sharyn found it difficult to find projects for the visiting groups. Coordinating everything and being sure the materials needed were on site, on time, and within the skill sets of the "workers" took lots of time. Setting up transportation and requesting things needing to be brought from the States by each visiting group also required time.

But the groups were enthused. They were delighted to be building fish ponds, passing buckets of concrete from Haitian to American to Haitian along long lines from the road down to the pouring sites, laughing and straining, learning a bit about the culture, and enjoying real Haitian food prepared over wood fires.

Hosting workgroups easily took more than 50% of Rodney and Sharyn's time. And the groups wanted to be with the Haitians, not working on fixing up the Lakil facility. That was possible, but it was secondary to the work in the hills.

Because it was important that people experience the mission and culture, long evening sessions occurred when groups were there. Questions were asked, answered, and most importantly, put into the Haitian cultural context. This was a huge energy drain for the Babes.

Beginning in 2003, as noted, four young people came for expected year-long assignments. Although these interns would live and work in the mountains, one prime purpose was to have them help in hosting mission visitors. Rodney and Sharyn would still be the official hosts, but spreading the functions, particularly when they were out in the project, freed up time for the Babes.

This was rudely interrupted in February 2004 when political crises and riots caused the four interns to escape on the last commercial flight out of Haiti. Just as the program was off to a good start, it had stopped—no mission groups, no interns, no hosting. The interns had not yet been fully trained.

Making Progress in the Face of Changes in PCUSA and Episcopal Diocese of Haiti

The existing arrangement between PCUSA and EEH called for them to cooperate in specific mission areas—healthcare, agriculture, education, plus services for the Haitian diaspora in the USA, exchange visits, and presbytery partnerships.

Agricultural considerations included CODEP and St. Barnabas in Terre Rouge. However, it was less clear how the exchange visits and presbytery partnerships would impact CODEP. This was an important consideration as the load on Rodney and Sharyn continued to grow.

Two other considerations loomed large: PCUSA indicated funding for the denomination was becoming an issue. It was not unique to the PCUSA; other mainline denominations faced the same issue. No one knew how this would affect CODEP.

These funding issues soon had their impact. First, Louisville began talking about a change in assignment for Rodney and Sharyn. The rationale was that their skills could better be utilized all over Haiti rather than only with CODEP. Not only that, but if the Babes were to leave CODEP, there were no funds to pay the salaries of their replacements.

This led to the other consideration: Bishop Duracin was saying all funding to CODEP should include a 10% across the board fee that would go directly to the Diocese of Haiti.* This was a significant amount of money, as spending at that time was about $350,000, so a $35,000 haircut would not be easy. And, as usual, the bishop hadn't asked directly but through the PCUSA.

Minutes of HFI Executive Board Meeting—First Presbyterian Church, New Bern, NC, February 14, 2003.

The bishop's request to get a percentage of CODEP funds, and the funding issues of both the Presbyterian and Episcopal denominations were troubling. This was a significant threat for Rodney and Sharyn, who, though burdened greatly by the load of work, had finally found a nice place to live in Haiti, safe and protected, at Lakil.

The beach outside the facility at Lakil at sunset. One look is enough to convince anyone that this comfortable, safe island of respite is the place to be in Haiti.

During their tenure with CODEP, they had been subject to removals because of political instability. Finally, at Lakil, they could withstand almost anything, and sometimes, in periods of political instability, it was more dangerous to travel to the airport in Port-au-Prince than it was to stay put at Lakil.

Losing Rodney and Sharyn would certainly cause significant problems in succession planning. And if their assignments were changed, HFI would have to find replacements and *pay for their salaries and benefits,* something that would complicate funding significantly.

Part of the PCUSA's discussions about changing the focus of mission coworkers was to have them do series of three-year assignments. While this was likely good, it included requiring missionaries to take a mandatory six-month sabbatical to return to the States for rest, relaxation, and "itineration."

Itineration was how mission coworkers connected with the larger Presbyterian denomination. Presbyteries and churches would know the schedules of missionaries, and they would visit to make presentations, preach, and answer questions. There was faith-building on both sides, and having a reasonably long period to do it was a wise decision.

For Rodney and Sharyn and CODEP, however, it was not easy to itinerate. They had been in the field for more than ten years, had been evacuated from Haiti several times, and finally had a safe, comfortable place to live in Haiti.

They did not want to move.

Accomplish Everything in the Face of Continuing Political Instability

It is important not to forget that the political situation in Haiti then was gradually deteriorating, as noted earlier. Aristide's second term regularly included intense political struggles, even if it was not always public or evident in the mountains. It was not specifically an outgrowth of Aristide's first-term troubles, but caution dictated that care should be taken.

By the end of 2004 the interim government appointed in Haiti following Aristide's resignation was beginning to fray. Initial actions by the United Nations set up a peacekeeping force. The UN once again named the Supreme Court Chief Justice, this time Boniface Alexandre, as interim president with a promise to hold democratic elections as soon as possible.

However, the interim government had not moved quickly to restore democracy. Elections still had not been held a year after Aristide left. The UN force was in place, and things were quiet. But the political undercurrents continued to simmer. No one knew when, or if, Aristide might return to reclaim his presidency.

But Rodney and Sharyn were safe at Lakil for the time being; Jamie Rhoads had returned, and few groups were coming, so at least the guest-hosting issue had subsided.

• • • • • •

It is reasonable to ask how the project fared during these times. Like most other situations the Haitian people face, they viewed it all stoically, keeping up the work and moving ahead. Gwo Mon was planting huge amounts of trees. A new area was being planted over the hill from Ti Apon. Fish ponds were producing fish, although with some difficulty.*

---

*Prior to 9-11-2001 visiting groups would check duffel bags packed with fish food, which was an important source of nutrition so the fish would grow to at least a half pound (about six to eight inches long). Now, duffel bags would not pass security, so CODEP's partner Bill Mebane, of the National Marine Biological Laboratory in Woods Hole, MA, suggested CODEP engage in photosynthetic methods of producing food for fish.

This involved creating aqua-composting in a corner of a pond, putting manure, leaves, and other organic materials into the soup of the loosely blocked compost area. Algae blooms would move into the larger pond and attach to bamboo "reeds" hung from cords into the water. The fish would then eat the algae, a nutritious food source, which in turn provided high-protein food for CODEP people.

This was a brilliant idea, and Bill even constructed a hothouse in cold Massachusetts to test the principles, which worked well. Because of differences between the two food sources, fish would not grow to quite the size that they had earlier. But as a food substitute, this was an elegant solution.

The results for 2004 were astounding in comparison with early years in the project. For example, after 2003 (after Gwo Mon had gotten off to a good start in 2002) the thirty working lakous planted an *average of 1,700 to 2,500 trees per day* during the planting season. Even planting during two short periods each year, annual trees planted amounted to well over 600,000 trees per year.

But results were more than just the specifics of targeted planting/ harvesting objectives. The people in CODEP were being led by animators who were growing in responsibility and skill. The project had continued through all the political disruptions and the sudden withdrawals of Rodney and Sharyn. Although issues continued between HFI and the PCUSA/Episcopal Diocese, they seemed not to have any substantial impact on the project and its growth.

No one knew, however, whether CODEP would falter if neglected for long periods. It was still the shining example of how agricultural development work could progress, grow, and significantly improve the lives and health of the participants directly. It also helped entire communities around the project indirectly.

One board member put it this way: "When we first went up the hill to see the project, all the little kids had red hair and potbellies (evidence of malnutrition) and wore tatters for clothes and had no shoes. Now, hardly any have red hair, and most are clothed well and all have shoes. Amazing."

• • • • • •

Now, with the changes in mission focus (the PCUSA used the term *missiology*), there was a good chance that Rodney and Sharyn would have to move from Lakil. Succession planning now became the focus at board meetings.

Rodney and Sharyn participated in discussions about succession planning. They participated in the conversations, but it was not an easy situation for them. Board members were sympathetic but likely did not realize how difficult it was for the Babes to have to listen as their future was being discussed openly before them, knowing that HFI wouldn't have much to say if the PCUSA decided to change their assignment.

But it is certainly clear that, from the Babes' perspective, it would be much better if the board decided to pay their salary and benefits so they no longer would be dependent on the PCUSA. But since they had a lot of years and funds vested in the PCUSA pension plan, it was unlikely that HFI could begin to match it.

Also, Rodney would retire in 2011, just a few years away, and if he retired with a full pension, he would be able to continue health insurance for life—another thing HFI could not afford.

The notion of development mission and the special focus it required was clear to the board. However, most board members didn't understand cultural nuances in CODEP, how the Haitians needed to be treated, and in particular how they might completely misinterpret board members' good intentions.

In the meantime, Jn Sémé Alexandre was a growing problem. He was the longest-term CODEP employee. He had built great interest "over the mountain" in Gwo Mon. He had three experienced animators who were willing to assist—Bastien Aimè, Madame Enese (Inez) Medeè, and Renè Decimè.

Jn Sémé had some ideas of his own. He worked with Jack and various board members about developing Haitian leaders. He wanted to use donated Bibles for a literacy program. These things were not new; Rodney had been saying much the same thing and had also encouraged leaders to take the initiative.

It is not clear why or when, but Jn Sémé began to challenge Rodney in several areas: making decisions in Gwo Mon, distributing fertilizer and plastic bags, and not reporting results. It soon became a power struggle that Jn Sémé exploited whenever possible when board members and guests visited.

Thus, board members became unwitting pawns in the struggle, as Sémé learned how to seek them out when they would be out in the project. (Usually without Rodney, who because of his earlier accident simply was not able to walk the long distances required to get to Gwo Mon.)

One of the most popular trips was to walk down to La Ferrier to see the wonder of the demonstration plot, located at the foot of Gwo Mon along the main path. Jn Sémé knew this, and would often meet board members there. He spoke French. So could some board members, so Jn Sémé could talk to them.

He would ask for plastic bags, fertilizer, and tools. Unsuspecting board members would agree to call Jim Pease in the States to get action on whatever "crisis" Jn Sémé brought up. Sometimes this was done without telling Rodney, who was infuriated, as anyone would be.

The broader situation regarding the Babes' assignments grew more and more grave during the latter part of 2004. Everyone had good intentions, but there were disagreements as to how to proceed. The problems grew instead of being resolved. Other entities controlled many events. Resolving many of them depended on the whims of the PCUSA in Louisville and the bishop in Haiti.

Because of this, Jim Pease increasingly felt it was becoming more and more difficult for him to function effectively. Bylaws were changed and the board was learning its new role. The project was growing. But still many unknowns remained as to how the three organizations fit together.

During this period, the board began to diverge from within. There were those who were asking the question, "Do we support the mission, or do we support the missionary?" It was a clear reference to having to make a choice between the project and the Babes, who managed it. It was a significant issue for the board.

Other organizations controlled many HFI and CODEP decisions. The HFI board got better at wrestling with decisions but still hadn't fully accepted their new roles. Mission versus missionary was dividing them. All these were signals to Jim that the board needed a push to gain full functionality.

Because of all these things, and after much prayer and soul-searching, Jim Please wrote a letter of resignation. He was reluctant to do this, but he explained he felt it would be in the best interests of the board and CODEP if he were no longer executive director.

At the next board meeting in January of 2005, several board members resigned, Jim Pease included. Since the PCUSA had finally decided that Rodney and Sharyn would be taking a six-month sabbatical beginning in August, the board passed several resolutions related to that, even though Rodney and Sharyn were not at the meeting. The annual board meeting was set for February 5th, a month later and on a Saturday when Rodney and Sharyn would be in the US and could attend.

At the February annual meeting, long-term board member Lars Bergstrom was elected as board chairman, replacing Lawson Drinkard, who had resigned. Also, Lars was appointed interim executive director until they could find a suitable replacement for Jim Pease. A search committee was formed to find an executive director, with a target completion date of June 1.

In March of 2005, with the search team in operation, Rodney and Sharyn went back to Haiti, having completed PCUSA obligations in the states. Jamie Rhoads had returned, and one of two new interns, Meredith Barkley, was in place at Lakil to learn the language. Another one, April Leese, would come from Pittsburgh Theological Seminary in May for the summer.

• • • • • •

Haiti Fund's search team was making progress, and on the 10th of May 2005, I was called as the new executive director of Haiti Fund. My first step was to contact Rodney to arrange to visit them in Lakil so I could start learning about this fascinating project. I was scheduled to fly down on June 14th, a Tuesday. It would be great—I'd meet Rodney and Sharyn and visit the project with them.

I could also meet Meredith Barkley and April Leese and reconnect with Jamie Rhoads (my presbytery youth council friend from ten years earlier). And finally I'd get a chance to meet some of the Haitians whose names I had heard and read about—Clement, Edvy, Jn Sémé, and others.

On Monday night, June 13th, instead of packing my bags for my first trip to Haiti, I was on the phone with American Airlines getting tickets for Meredith, Jamie, April, Rodney, and Sharyn to come out once again. The political situation had deteriorated considerably, and the PCUSA was pulling all the missionaries from Haiti, our entire group included.

The sabbatical, it seemed, had started early. Rodney and Sharyn would not be authorized to return to Haiti until September 2006. Their assignments would be changed by the PCUSA and the EEH well into their sabbatical. They would have to move to Port-au-Prince.

CODEP would continue digging, germinating, planting, and harvesting.

But the world around CODEP, it seemed, was exploding.

Revision, Re-Vision, and Growth During Upheaval

At this juncture of CODEP's history, there were significant structural issues. Both the visionary and the project designer were no longer working in the project. No Americans were in Haiti, so Rodney had set up a mechanism to ensure the flow of funds through Edvy.

And Rodney had wisely done some housecleaning before he left. He had known he would take a six-month sabbatical beginning August 1. He did not know it would start early—in mid-June. But he knew he had to deal with Jn Sémé before he left because the risk was too great to leave him in place.

At the animator meeting at the beginning of June, Jn Sémé once again failed to turn in reports of Gwo Mon activities. He had withheld them since the prior August—insisting that he be named the director of Gwo Mon CODEP, reporting to Jim Pease and the HFI board of directors. By now, Jn Sémé had four subordinates—Bastien, Madame Enese, René and Carlo. Rodney pointedly asked them to turn in their reports, but they did not do so.

In a planned strategy of confrontation, just as the meeting began, Rodney fired Jn Sémé for insubordination—failure to follow the rules, specifically to report on Gwo Mon activities for an extended period. He expelled Sémé from the meeting. Then Rodney announced he would leave the meeting too.

Further, he would return in five minutes. If the reports were not turned in by the time he returned, any animator whose reports were not there would be fired, just like Jn Sémé.

When he returned, all four reports were there. The insurrection had been stemmed.

• • • • • •

It is easy to look back on this incident and wonder about its importance. But the project was at significant risk for a variety of reasons, and a misstep of any kind could spell the end of what, to that point, had been a magnificent success. Among those risks were:

- no continuity of leadership assured—either at CODEP or HFI
- no apparent consensus among HFI, EEH, and PCUSA about CODEP's continuing role in Haiti
- the bishop wanting 10% of CODEP's disbursed funds to go to EEH
- the recent conflict on the HFI board and no guarantee that things were better than before
- a new executive director with no experience with CODEP or Haiti
- the recent power struggle in CODEP with Jn Sémé and no longer having his leadership skills
- PCUSA changing mission focus for their missionaries, de-emphasizing project assignments
- uncertainty as to how long the PCUSA personnel would be kept out of Haiti
- not knowing whether they would change Rodney and Sharyn's assignment, or when
- if that were to happen, HFI would be required to pay salary and benefits for new missionaries
- still no compelling strategy for use of the guesthouse and visiting mission groups

Volume II of this series tells how CODEP has been able to overcome these significant issues that threatened its very existence. It has not been easy. It is a fascinating story of risk, faith, courage, and entrepreneurial spirit. Clearly, it could not have been done without the continuing commitment and hard work of the people of CODEP.

John V. Winings
January 2016

Appendix I—Chronology

Throughout both volumes of this book, there were always multiple events occurring contemporaneously. These need to be viewed in context with each other, even if they are separated geographically, functionally, and organizationally. Thus, from this perspective, and for reference, here are some of the major dates that flag for you the narrative that unfolds in the volumes of this book:

1982 – Jack Hanna's retirement

1983 – Merger agreement between Presbyterian Church in the US and the United Presbyterian Church—called the Presbyterian Church (USA)

1987 – Project work in Jamaica

1988 – Visit to Bigonè and initial presentation to farmers about gardens

1989 – Formation of project work group headed by Père Racine

1990 – Project realignment with committee changes; Racine takes charge

1991 – Rodney Babe started working for CDP; lived in Léogâne

1991 – Overthrow of Aristide; Babes evacuated to the US; institution of US/UN embargo of Haiti

1992 – Babes return to Port-au-Prince; project restart; progress in tree planting, cisterns, food supply

1993 – Reestablishment of Aristide regime; gradual relaxation of rationing

1995 – Installation of new Episcopal bishop; exchange rate deteriorates

1996 – Renè Preval elected president following Aristide

1997 – Begin filling swamp and construction of living quarters/guesthouse Lakil

2000 – Jack Hanna retires as president of Haiti Fund; strategic and succession plans developed

2001 – Haiti Fund's first executive director hired

2003 – Four Volunteers-In-Mission join CODEP for yearlong assignments

2004 – Political upheaval—Aristide abdicates in February; CODEP personnel leave, only the Babes and Jamie return

2005 – More political upheaval; author called as executive director; missionaries evacuated

2006 – Rodney/Sharyn Babe transferred to Port-au-Prince by PCUSA

2006 – Rick/Kathy Land become interim directors of CODEP

2009 – Rick and Kathy Land retire; new resident leadership begins

2010 – Massive earthquake devastates Haiti; new people resign; author moves to Haiti

2011 – CODEP begins to chart its future; movement toward increased leadership by animators

2012 – CODEP moves toward sustainability

2013 – CODEP 2 begins, a significant growth statement by CODEP

2014 – HFI evicted from missionary residence/guesthouse at Lakil

2015 – Residence quarters relocated to Duklo, now located in the middle of CODEP land area

Appendix II—Glossary

ADRA – Adventist Development & Relief Association, an organization chartered by the Canadian International Development Authority (CIDA) to provide supplemental food (rice and cooking oil) to peasant farmers in Haiti during the period following the coup d'état in 1992

Agwonòme – Kreyòl word for a person knowledgeable in agriculture; one who has a certificate in agriculture

Animators – the leadership group in CODEP—shown generally in order of the responsibility they have—their names are:

> Edvy Durandice – an animator since the early days, currently member of the Office of the Director of CODEP, manages the administrative functions of CODEP

> Clement Tercelin – also a member of CODEP from the beginning, currently a member of the Office of the Director of CODEP and who manages all the logistical functions of CODEP

> Bastien Aimè, – a long-term animator, originally responsible for four groups in Gwo Mon when it began, a graduate of St. Barnabas and who has a certificate as an agwonòme. He currently is the leader of the CODEP depot effort to assist CODEP members to have a place to sell their CODEP products.

> Carlo Cenat – animator for several years; originally had groups in Gwo Mon and works with Bastien to manage the depot

> Madame Enese Medeé – a long-term animator and one of three who manage the CODEP depot and who is an officer in APKF, the agriculture cooperative formed by Edvy, which is a supply store as well as service place for microcredit loans

René Decimé – a long-term animator who works in Gwo Mon and has become the main person who assists with construction projects

Jn Claude Barthelemy – one of the original animators, who works in both Cormier and Fonde Boudin and who is also an officer of APKF

Madame Elyseé Saintfleurant – an original animator, comes from DeLouch, and who has three groups, but has also sponsored several new groups in the past few years

Berton Kercelin – a graduate of St. Barnabas and an animator for several years who manages groups over the hill on the Jacmel Road, which opens up new territory in that area

Venus Cerant – an animator for ten years; works in areas of Ti Apon

Jenner Cenat – a St. Barnabas graduate and animator for about eight years; has groups in Ti Apon

Theofil Sainfleur – a young animator, graduate of St. Barnabas, and an agwonòme; has groups in Palmist Avan section of CODEP

Elerder Brioche – a new animator, but a long time CODEP participant as a chèf ekip; works with groups in Palmist Avan

Marie Claire Saintini – a new animator, she is extremely capable and creative; works in Palmist Avan

Lénonce Desiré – a new animator; lives and works in Citwonye, one of the most distant reaches of CODEP; very creative and competent

Jean Rico – a new animator; works in DeLouch area

APKF – Asosyasyon Paysan Kormye Fondeboudin—the farmers' cooperative for Cormier and Fonde Boudin run by Edvy Durandice

April Leese – an intern who served starting May 2005 but was evacuated three weeks later

Bishop Duracin – the Episcopal Bishop of the Haiti Diocese

Bwa Goch – one of the forest zones of CODEP, situated on the left branch of the Cormier river, where Jamie Rhoads lived, and near both the demonstration forest and Gwo Mon

Cédras (Joseph Raoul Cédras) – the titular head of Haiti after Jean-Bertrand Aristide was deposed in a coup d'état in 1991; he relinquished power later, and Aristide was restored and finished his term

Christianville – a mission project east of Léogâne, which has a school, fish ponds, and several agriculture projects. It also has residences where Rodney and Sharyn lived for a few years.

Clark Scalera – a VIM and intern from August 2003 until evacuated in February 2004; chose not to return in May of 2004 since he only had a short time to finish his assignment

CODEP – Cormier Development Project; later renamed Comprehensive Development Project after it moved into several additional watersheds

Contour canals – ditches dug along the contour of a hill, built to retain water; held in place by stabilizing grass planted on the lower side; they retain moisture and form a natural compost when leaves fall off trees planted above the ditch (or canal)

Coppice – a method of cutting trees off at the trunk, causing them to grow many shoots; also a plant that regrows after it is cut down in much the same manner. Eucalyptus trees planted by CODEP do this, as do some other species of forest tree.

Cormier River – the watershed leading from Anba Tonel to the ocean, and flowing along the Jacmel road and near Kafou Dufort

Darbonne – a city southeast of Leyogàn, where government health offices are located

Duklo – the name of the area in the center of the CODEP project where APKF and CODEP's depot is located

Dures – Pastor Dures, formerly an animator, he is a schoolmaster and farmer as well as the pastor of a nondenominational church called Siloe (sill-oh-way)

ECHO – Educational Concerns for Hunger Organization, a North Ft. Myers, FL, organization dedicated to doing research in tropical plants, animals, and agricultural systems for improving the lives and conditions under which many farmers throughout the world work and live

ERD – Episcopal Relief and Development—the relief and development arm of the Episcopal Church in the United States, located in New York

Father (Père) Racine – the priest who originally headed the committee to study how to go about getting CODEP started

Frank and Becca Harmon – Interns who came to Haiti in October of 2003, planning to stay for a year

FURREC – Civil Reconstruction and Emergency Fund, the organization (along with MEDA and OIM) that provided grants for paying wages for needed work during the early 1990s

Gwo kay – literally "large house" with a footprint of 27 square meters, with two rooms and a porch on one end

Gwo Mon – literally "large mountain" where population density was low and where vast areas of reforestation could occur; this area was opened up by Jn Sémé

Haiti Fund, Inc. – US-based 501 C (3) not-for-profit charitable organization whose sole benefactor is CODEP

Hôpital Ste. Croix (HSC) – the Episcopal hospital in Léogâne whose long history included support of government health care initiatives, PCUSA support, and had a guesthouse on the grounds that housed early CODEP visitors

Interns or Volunteers In Mission (VIM) – the PCUSA term for young people (mostly) who would work for no salary and spend from three months to more than a year in various countries, Haiti included, and CODEP specifically

Itineration – a term used by the PCUSA for activities done by missionaries when they come to the US for breaks from their foreign work. When they itinerate, they visit churches and presbyteries to talk about their mission and the culture of the country.

Jack Hanna – the founder and visionary who started Haiti Fund, Inc. and the Comprehensive Development Project in Haiti

Jack Stoner – a builder from Charlottesville, VA, who designed the original gwo kay, assisted in building Lakil guesthouse, and who was the founder of one of HFI's major partners, Building Goodness Foundation

Jacmel – a resort on the south coast of Haiti reachable by RN 202 (Route Nationale 202), which runs through the center of the CODEP project

Jamie Rhoads – an intern (VIM) who lived in Bwa Goch for two years beginning in 2003 while working in CODEP; he later returned to Haiti and lived in Cap Haitien for five years and is a board member of HFI.

Jim Pease – Executive Director of HFI from 2001–2005

Jim Sylivant – long-term board member of HFI and troubleshooting specialist who is an electrical engineer; speaks Kreyòl and fluent French

John Thienpont – on-site manager of the Lakil construction; lived in Haiti at Lakil for a year

Jn Claude Cerin – Haitian director of MEDA during its involvement in Haiti

Jn Sémé Alexandrè – first employee of CODEP, from 1989, and developer of La Ferrier demonstration forest and Gwo Mon zone of reforestation

Kafou – a western suburb of Port-au-Prince (also spelled Carrefour in French) where Jn Sémé lived and commuted to and from CODEP from each day

La Ferrier – site of the CODEP demonstration forest, about a mile north of the Jacmel road and on a site visible from several locations along the road

Lakil – location of the CODEP guesthouse facility, missionary residence, and self-contained power, water, fish hatchery, and propane utilities

Lakou – a small community in Haiti consisting of several houses and typically having from twenty-five to fifty people in residence. These communities were the basic unit of CODEP's development effort. Only a lakou could join CODEP, not individuals within it. These communities typically have access to land for reforestation.

Land tenure – the term for who has ownership, use, and access to land in Haiti. In the legal system, land tenure is a confused and unclear system so that rights are conferred on owners, renters, and occupiers.

Lars Bergstrom – president of Haiti Fund, Inc. board from 2005–2009 and long-time visitor to Haiti

Laurent Dubois – Professor of linguistics and history at Duke University, specialist in Haiti, and author of the well-reviewed book, *Haiti: The Aftershocks of History*, Metropolitan Books, Henry Holt, LLC, 2012, New York, 2012

Legliz Epifane – the Episcopal Parish located near the guesthouse/missionary residence facility at Lakil

Léogâne – (in Kreyòl, Leyogàn) a medium-sized city located thirty-five miles west of Port-au-Prince, Haiti. Léogâne is a political center, a *komin* (county), and is where Hôpital Ste. Croix is located, as well as a well-known nursing school, many schools, and was the center of the reconstruction effort outside Port-au-Prince following the 2010 earthquake; Léogâne lost a significant percentage of its homes, and a massive rebuilding effort followed.

Leon Dorleans – leader of Haiti Outreach Ministries in Blanchard and Cite Soleil, Haiti. He is a minister who has built several congregations in one of the most poverty-stricken areas of Haiti and has medical clinics and schools as part of the ministry to the poor; he has been a long friend of CODEP and assisted in getting the interns out of Haiti in the political upheaval at the end of February 2004.

Madame Jacques – one of CODEP's leaders, called a chèf ekip, who lives in Gwo Mon, overlooking Leyogàn in the distance

Madame Davide – the first DeLouch resident to offer her land for reforestation, beginning in 1990

Madame Philip – also a chèf ekip, who lives in Bwa Goch and who provided her incentive gwo kay as Jamie Rhoads's home for two years

MBL – Marine Biological Laboratory in Woods Hole, MA. Their efforts and the efforts of Bill Mebane, who manages one of the main ichthyology research laboratories there, was instrumental in aiding CODEP to provide productive fish ponds as a source of food protein for CODEP members

Bill Mebane – Manager of one of Marine Biological Laboratory's research labs in Woods Hole, MA

MEDA – Mennonite Economic Development Associates, a private nonprofit Canadian institution that had a program sponsored by the Canadian International Development Authority (CIDA) which managed microcredit loans in Haiti and specifically in the CODEP area

MINUSTAH – MINUSTAH (United Nations Stabilisation Mission in Haiti; in French, Mission des Nations Unies pour la Stabilisation en Haïti) is a 5,000–9,000-member task force of peacekeeping troops; they have been deployed in Haiti since 1994, reauthorized in 2004 at the time of Aristide's abdication during his second term as president of Haiti

New Bern – a city in southeastern North Carolina located close to the Intercoastal Waterway where Jack Hanna founded Haiti Fund, Inc. in 1989

NGO – acronym for nongovernmental organization; this includes large and small organizations, from the Red Cross and Samaritan's Purse all the way to NGOs even smaller than CODEP.

Norplant – the brand name of contraceptive implants for birth control used in Haiti through Hôpital Ste. Croix in Haiti from 1991–2000, when they discontinued service

OIM – Organisation Internationale pour les Migrations, which conducts programs to relocate and democratize displaced persons; in Haiti they worked to assist in erosion control, aiding community grassroots organizations, and food storage such as grain

PCUSA – Presbyterian Church (USA), formed by the combination (in 1983) of the Presbyterian Church in the United States (PCUS) and the United Presbyterian Church (UPC); PCUS was headquartered in Atlanta, UPC in New York, and the combination chose Louisville, KY, as the new headquarters, where it remains today

Pepinyè – tree nursery, where seeds are germinated in plastic bags and watered until they are big enough to be planted; pepinyès typically have a source of water nearby and have a compost pit where manure and good soil are mixed and composted prior to being used as fill for plastic bags

Pikliz – a spicy coleslaw used as a dressing for many Haitian foods

Primogeniture – the system of inheritance common in European monarchies, where the eldest son inherited the entire estate; post-revolutionary France, and thence Haiti, adopted the alternate method, which was to have all family members inherit the estate equally; this led to property ownership and land tenure being a significant problem in Haiti, as any piece of land typically has many owners

Renè Preval – President of Haiti following Jn-Bertrand Aristide both in the late 1990s and in 2005; he served two five-year terms

Robert D. Lupton – the author of *Toxic Charity*, a well-reviewed book that exposes the present-day practices of charitable giving and mission trips

Rodney and Sharyn Babe – the first missionaries who developed CODEP; Rodney is credited with establishing the system that re-sulted in CODEP's astounding success as an agricultural develop-ment project

Rouyonne River – one of two main rivers that drain the mountains south of Léogâne; the other is the Momence, which has a source near the Rouyonne, but which drains east of Léogâne

Stipend – a small daily wage, paid at the end of the month, which origi-nally was set up by CODEP as a compensatory favor following the ceasing of the ADRA food distribution program

Tap-tap – a taxi made from a pickup truck that has a roof and two bench seats inside that is a common form of public transportation in Hai-ti; it derives its name from people who wish to get off by tapping the side of the truck, which then stops, lets them off, and takes the fare

Tonton Macoute – a secret service organization used by the Duvaliers during their regimes, having the reputation of significant abuse of human rights

USAID – United States Agency for International Development—an or-ganization created by Congress which does development projects throughout the world; one complaint is that, by law, all of the ma-terials used in the project must be obtained from US suppliers of goods and services, which shuts out local vendors in the recipient countries

Vetiver – a strong-smelling stabilizing grass used for erosion control on contour canals

Wozo – a bamboo-like stabilizing grass used for erosion control on contour canals, preferred by many farmers because in addition to having good root systems, also provides long leaves that can be harvested and fed to animals

Wyeth Pharmaceuticals – the US distributor and seller of Norplant contraceptive devices which were used by Hôpital Ste. Croix and CODEP for women in the CODEP project area

Appendix III—Bibliography

Abbot, Elizabeth. *Haiti: The Duvaliers and Their Legacy.* New York: Simon & Schuster, 1991.

Anderson, Genny. "Bottom Dwellers, Ch. 4.1.1, Coral Reef Formation." *Marine Science* (2003).

Bonenfant, Jacques L. "History of Haitian-Creole: From Pidgin to Lingua Franca and English Influence on the Language." *Review of Higher Education and Self-Learning (REHSL)* 4 (June 2011): 27–34.

Casley, Dennis J. and Lury, Denis A. *A Technical Supplement to Monitoring and Evaluation of Agriculture and Rural Development Projects.* "Estimating Crop Production in Development Projects: Methods and Their Limitations." Poate, C. D. and Casley, Dennis J. Washington, DC: THE WORLD BANK, 1985.

Coupeau, Steeve. *History of Haiti.* (Greenwood Series of the Modern Nations). Westwood, CT: Greenwood Press, 2007.

Dubois, Laurent. *Haiti: The Aftershocks of History,* New York: Metropolitan Books, Henry Holt, LLC, 2012.

Elmer. Duane H. *Cross-Cultural Conflict: Building Relationships for Effective Ministry.* Downers Grove, IL: InterVarsity Press, 1993.

Farmer, Paul M. *The Uses of Haiti,* Monroe, ME: Common Courage Press, 2005.

Girard, Philip R. "Operation Restore Democracy?" *Journal of Haitian Studies* 8, no. 2 (2002): 70.

Haggerty, Richard A. ed., *Haiti: A Country Study.* "Land Tenure and Land Policy." Washington: GPO for the Library of Congress, 1989.

Hall, Holly. "Americans Rank 13th in Charitable Giving Among Countries Around the World." *The Chronicle of Philanthropy.* Washington, DC, December 23, 2013.

Hallward, Peter. *Damming the Flood: Haiti, Aristide, and the Politics of Containment.* London: Verso Books, 2007.

Katz, Jonathan M. *The Big Truck That Went By: How the World Came to Save Haiti and Left Behind a Disaster.* New York: Palgrave Macmillan, 2013.

Kidder, Tracy. *Mountains Beyond Mountains*. New York: Random House Publishing Group, 2003.

Kushner, Jacob. "Who Owns What in Haiti?" *The New Yorker*. January 28, 2015.

Lupton, Robert D. *TOXIC CHARITY: How Churches and Charities Hurt Those They Help (And How to Reverse It)*. New York: Harper Collins, 2011.

McAlister, Elizabeth A. *Rara! Vodou, Power, and Performance in Haiti and its Diaspora*. University of California Press, 2002.

Montgomery-Fate, Tom. *Beyond the White Noise—Mission in a Multicultural World*. St. Louis, MO: Chalice Press, 1997

Murray, Andrew. *Humility: The Journey Toward Holiness*. New York: Anson D. F. Randolph & Co, 1895.

Ng Cheong-Lum, Roseline and Jermyn, Leslie. *Haiti*. New York: Marshall Cavendi, 2005.

Perlmann, Peter and Troye-Blomberg, Marita. *Malaria Immunology*. "Malaria and the Immune System in Humans." Basel, Karger. *Chemical Immunology* (magazine) 80 (2002): 229–242.

Reitherman, Robert. *Earthquakes and Engineers: An International History*. Reston, VA: ASCE Press, 2012. pp. 208–209.

Suzata, Eriko. "Education in Haiti: An Overview of Trends, Issues, and Plans." *World Innovative Summit for Education. (W.I.S.E.)*. Qatar (2011).

Umpleby, Stuart A., *METHODS FOR COMMUNITY DEVELOPMENT: THE WORK OF THE INSTITUTE OF CULTURAL AFFAIRS* Department of Management Science, The George Washington University, Washington, DC 20052.

Wheatley, Margaret J., *Leadership and the New Science: Discovering Order in a Chaotic World*. Oakland, CA: Berrett-Koehler Publishers, Inc., 2006.

Wilentz, Amy. *The Rainy Season: Haiti Since Duvalier*. New York: Simon and Schuster, 1989.

___. "ADRA in Haiti." http://www.ADRAHaiti.org.ht/history.html.

___. *Chapter 4: Minimum Standards in Shelter, Settlement, and non-Food Items, Medicine, Conflict and Survival*. "Mortality, crime and access to basic needs before and after the Haiti earthquake." International Federation of Red Cross and Red Crescent Societies 26, no. 4 (2010). http://www.ifrc.org/PageFiles/95884/D.01.02.a.%20 SPHERE%20Chap.%204-%20shelter%20and%20NFIs_%20English.pdf.

___. "Coral Reef Formation." *Marine Science.* http://www.marinebio.net/ marinescience/04benthon/crform.htm,

___. "Education: Overview." United States Agency for International Development. 2007.

___. "Haiti." *The World Factbook*, 2011. Central Intelligence Agency.

___. "Hôpital Ste. Croix in Léogâne." *Episcopal Medical Missions Foundation.* http://www.emmf.com/hscroix.htm. Austin, Texas.

___. "India project." 1976. http://www.ica-usa.org/?page=history.

___. "Languedoc Property Inheritance Law." http://www.midi-france. info/0814_inheritance.htm.

___. "Léogâne" https://en.wikipedia.org/wiki/L%C3%A9og%C3%A2ne.

___. "MedWatch – New safety information summaries 2000—Norplant." FDA (September 13, 2000).

___. "National Center for Charitable Statistics, Household Giving as a Percentage of Total Giving." *Giving USA 2013: The Annual Report on Philanthropy for the Year 2012.*

___. "National Center for Charitable Statistics, Household Giving as a Percentage of Total Giving." 2011 IRS Statistics of Income file, "*Individual Complete Report (Publication 1304)*." Table 2.1.

___. "Potential Charitable Giving in Emerging Economies." http://www. philanthropynews.alliancemagazine.org/2013-world-giving-index-shows-potential-of-charitable-giving-in-emerging-economies/.

___. "What Causes Surface Winds, Mountain Winds and Anabatic Winds." http://belfortinstrument.com/causes-surface-winds-mountain-winds-anabatic-winds/. Belfort Instrument Company, Baltimore, MD.

___. "World Giving Index—Methodology." https://brainthing.wordpress. com/2010/11/29/world-giving-index-methodology.

Please understand that sometimes Internet links expire and may no longer work. Should this be the case with any of these above, I apologize for that.

Appendix IV—Index

Discussion Questions/Topics

1. The Footpath . . .

- How would you react to the taxi ride to the domestic airport in Port-au-Prince?
- When you contemplate taking such a trip, what fears, if any, cross your mind?
- How would you have reacted with your flashlight, relieving yourself in the dark?

2. Jack Hanna, the Visionary

- How would you do community-building like Jack did in Jamaica, but in the USA?
- What were the issues surrounding getting sixteen communities to have a common purpose?
- Why was Jack able to leave the Jamaica project so early? What could have gone wrong?

3. Rodney Babe, the Designer

- Why do you suppose the reforestation assignment was so attractive?
- Talk about the travel conditions during the embargo and how you might react.
- What is your view of government instability in countries like Haiti?

4. Finding Haitian Leaders

- How would you have chosen leaders for CODEP, after the Madame Davide meeting?
- How would your spirit flag (or would it) if you had to be removed from Haiti from time to time like Rodney and Sharyn?
- Do you accept the rationale given for USAID, MEDA, FUR-REC, and other programs and how they ended late in the 1990s? Explain.

5. Clement, the Salesman

- How do you think you would have reacted if you couldn't go to school till you were twelve, like Clement?

- How would you describe Clement's personality?
- Can you compare his perspective and work ethic with anyone you know in the States? Explain.

6. *The Steep Learning Curve to Success*

- Discuss your view of the institution of the stipend and how it worked; discuss how you would stop it.
- What about the institution of incentives to get the focus more long term?
- How would you choose the ten animators, if not using Rodney's methods?
- How would you solve the land tenure problem, if renting were not available?

7. *Edvy, the Banker*

- Would you make an investment in a treadle sewing machine like Edvy? Why or why not?
- In your neighborhood or hometown, could you be a credit representative like Edvy? Why or why not?
- What culture differences, if any, are there here in the US that preclude doing microcredit loans?

8. *Responding to Donor Interest*

- What is your view of a mission trip? Explain.
- How does development differ from relief in your view?
- Where do you, or where does your church stand, on mission discovery trips?
- Do they work? Why or why not?

9. *Edvy's Challenge*

- Would you say that Haiti's culture is very different from ours with respect to attitudes toward cancer?
- What would you do if you had to live for several months, isolated from your family with little means of communication, and facing cancer, like Edvy?
- How would you have improved on the decision taken by the board of HFI regarding Edvy's treatment? Explain.

10. Building Lakil

- Would you have started with filling the swamp, or would you have sought another location?
- What do you think of the long-term contract between Jack Hanna and the bishop regarding the property?
- Which of the criteria for designing the CODEP facility at Lakil would you consider not necessary? Explain.
- Are there other design criteria not included you would add? Explain.

11. Expanding to Gwo Mon

- Explain your view of the strategy behind building the demonstration forest.
- Explain whether you think it is justified to do "special" fertilizing, weeding, and side-dressing of trees in La Ferrier when other areas didn't get the same amounts.
- What in your view is attractive about developing Gwo Mon; and how Jn Sémé led the effort?

12. Clement's Promotion

- Describe your reaction to the kinds of jobs Clement and his sister had in Port-au-Prince in the mid-eighties.
- What do you think of Clement having a wife that was eight years older than him?
- Would you have asked Clement to check out the work of other animators? Why or why not? Explain.

13. Forming APKF

- What do you think of the transition from MEDA to Fonkoze and then MEDA to APKF?
- Would you have wanted to do what Edvy did as he worked to form the organization?
- How does APKF tie to CODEP (if at all) and is this good or bad and why?
- The money returned to CODEP from MEDA was used for the animator loan program and to build the APKF building. What do you think of these practices?

14. The Interns Solution

- Many college kids today actively seek intern positions. Do you think they would still do so if the conditions were similar now to what they were in Haiti when the CODEP interns started?
- There were, including the Peace Corps volunteer, a total of seven interns who served in CODEP. Do you think this program received a fair trial? Why or why not?

15. Nwèl (Noel)

- Can you explain a situation in your life where you felt you had intruded on another person's culture (as when I asked Nwèl to write out her name, not knowing whether she could read/write)?
- What do you think of Haiti's emphasis on their kids getting an education as far as possible, knowing what you know about their educational standards?
- How would you go about keeping your kids from leaving and going to Port-au-Prince if you were a Haitian parent?
- Why do you think Nwèl was so reticent to talk about the death of her father and mother?

16. Organizational Challenges

- Do you agree that the reporting relationships that Rodney and Sharyn had were as difficult as I described them? Why or why not?
- What do you think of how Rodney had to report to both the Bishop and the PCUSA while still doing HFI's work in Haiti in CODEP?
- What is your view of assigning missionaries to specific projects versus the kind of missiology that says that to work in a country is to immerse yourself in the culture and do work in the fashion of a partner, without taking a role as leader?
- (The question above assumes I have represented the missiology correctly—if not, please challenge it and explain why it is wrong.)

17. Changing of the Guard

- Do you agree with the several organizational changes made, and if not, how would you change things?
- What do you suppose caused the rift in the board of HFI? What would you have done to prevent it? Or, would you?
- How would you have managed the coming six-month sabbatical for the Babes, given the changes in the board occurring only seven months before they left?

Epilogue: Revision, Re-Vision, and Growth During Upheaval

- How would you have handled the Jn Sémé situation?
- Do you concur that the list of reasons constituted significant risks to HFI/CODEP?
- What do you think will be the keys to CODEP's revival and rejuvenation in the next period?

About the Author

John Winings came to his role as executive director of Haiti Fund, Inc. following a successful 40-year career in industry. His broad skills in science, marketing, manufacturing, technology transfer and top management uniquely qualify him to provide the kind of insights evident in this book.

After receiving his BS and MBA from the University of Illinois, John worked for Occidental Petroleum Corporation and The BOC Group before moving to North Carolina in 1990. Here he has been a turnaround specialist for venture capital firms with portfolio companies needing strong leadership and has served as a consultant to individuals and organizations needing renewed energy and focus.

A life-long Presbyterian, John has been an elder in the Presbyterian Church (USA) since 1978. He was a charter member of Wake Forest Presbyterian Church and is a Commissioned Ruling Elder who served two churches in New Hope Presbytery (North Eastern North Carolina), Butner Presbyterian Church and Clayton New Church Development. John was interim executive of the Synod of the Mid-Atlantic of the PCUSA from 2007–2008.

John was commissioned as the Executive Director of Haiti Fund, Inc. in 2005. Haiti Fund is a validated ministry of the Presbytery of New Hope. Following the earthquake in Haiti in 2010, John and his wife Debbie moved to Haiti where John took on the additional position of director of CODEP while continuing his Haiti Fund work. Since 2012, he has served with two Haitians (Edvy Durandice and Clement Tercelin) in the Office of the Director of CODEP, where the three of them share responsibilities as CEO.

John and Debbie live in Wake Forest, NC, and have three children and five grandchildren.

Connect with John at www.JohnWinings.com

54505710R00125

Made in the USA
Charleston, SC
06 April 2016